# FRANZ ZIEGLER

# MAGIC

# CHOCOLATE

This is how you can conjure up
original figures out of chocolate.
A specialised book for creative confectioners,
pastry-cooks and chocolate fans.
Includes 111 sweet creations
in 74 close-ups as well as 176 detailed
and work photos and important stencils
as facilitation of work in the annex.

Hugo Matthaes Druckerei und Verlag
GmbH & Co. KG

## Franz Ziegler Wishes to Thank Most Cordially

For its generosity, Max Felchlin Inc., which made the premises and the prefabricates available

Mr. C. Aschwanden for support during this project

Beat Herrmann and my colleagues Andy Mätzler, Anita Heiniger, Andrea Schürpf, Peter Bolliger
and Urs Kälin for moral support and a good workplace ambience

The good fairies of Condirama, Helen and Romy

Jean-Pierre and Evelyn König for their professional and smooth cooperation in photographing

Ralph Occhiodori for the creative logo

Keith Hurdman for meticulously proof-reading the manuscript

All of my professional colleagues who exerted a positive influence on me in my career

My wife Gaby, without whose energetic and moral support this book
would not exist today

Printed in Germany

Photos and cover picture: König & König, Zurich

Design: Erich Schönbach

Book production: Leonie von Sobbe

Editing: Hans-Peter Ritter

Overall production: Hugo Matthaes Druckerei und Verlag GmbH & Co. KG, Stuttgart

# Table of Contents

# PREFACE
## by Lars Johansson

*Magic Chocolate* is a special kind of book. It is not intended to be read from cover to cover like a novel, nor is it to be treated merely as a work of reference. Correctly used, *Magic Chocolate* can greatly facilitate pastry work and chocolate work, and be a source of knowledge and inspiration.

Many pastry chefs have become famous for original ideas introduced while working in hotels, restaurants and pastry shops. Most people look upon the outstanding pastry chef as an artist creating beauty and eye appeal in the preparation and presentation of centre-pieces and chocolate creations. It is said that beauty enriches goodness and health – qualities we all wish to possess.

To write a book containing formulas with practical instructions, directions and/or suggestions that can be readily understood and followed by anyone (professional or inexperienced) is by no means an easy task. Franz Ziegler has managed to do this!

The primary purpose of Franz Ziegler's book is to express ideas as clearly and concisely as possible.

His intention is to make a simple and practical chocolate creation to meet the needs of the pastry chef's imagination.

I believe that this is an outstanding book and should be treasured by all true pastry chefs. It belongs on every pastry chef's bookshelf.

My sincere congratulations to Franz Ziegler!

Lars Johansson
Director, International Baking and Pastry Institute
Johnson & Wales University

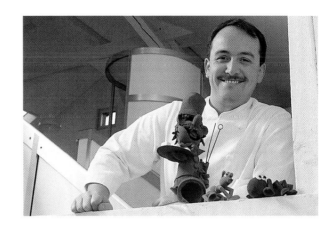

# FOREWORD

How did I come upon the idea of doing a book? Only a few years ago I was close to trading in my profession for a better paid office job. But the possibility of expressing myself in this wonderful profession, of always being able to learn and discover new things, was the main reason why I remained true to my calling. It is my hope that this book will impart to other confectioners something of the joy of creativity which I experience.

I found this enjoyment in colleagues. The evening lectures by Freddy Eggenschwiler and Erwin Lichtensteiger in the Trade College at Winterthur opened up dimensions for me which I had never dared to dream of. This suddenly provided that artistic part of this trade which can make it so wonderful.
I learned simple ways of being able to work effectively with marzipan. A cake decoration from then on became an enjoyable challenge and not a sheer immovable obstacle.

For that reason I practised alone at night with everything creative which this trade has to offer. Even today it is still immense fun for me to learn a new technique or a special form.

I soon had the opportunity of working in a company which cultivated the artistic aspect with as much love and pride as I did myself, and which is successful by doing so: in the Merz Pastry Shop in Chur. The unusually talented Andreas Cavegn proved then, as he still does today, that couverture work is no unprofitable art. I developed enormously in that period. A big step forward had been taken, into a future which made this book possible for me. A further step, and a great opportunity, was the chance to work for Felchlin as a travelling Pastry Chef. To travel to Japan, the US, Singapore and many other countries and to learn from professional attitudes predominant there, was an experience for which I am very grateful.

Without such experience, one would be repeating the same thing over and over again. In this way, new doors were constantly being opened up to let the tradesman expand his horizons.

And so I would like to express thanks to all those, with whose assistance and ideas I could continue my development, especially my parents, who consistently helped to advance my early career. Without their wise foresight and support this work would never have come about.

In a time, when everything is supposed to be done rationally, and, if possible, by machine, there must be room for a contrast: for the playful, in other words, for creativity – for something which binds young and old professional colleagues to their trade. Therefore, you should start tomorrow, to enjoy the fun of couvertures. You will discover that it brings amazing success.

Lots of luck and patience, yours

Franz Ziegler

## TECHNIQUES

When leafing through this book, you will encounter numerous techniques. The author, however, confined himself to 2 or 3 of these techniques per figure. Due to the great number of figures all important handling is talked about.

If you do not find the corresponding technique next to the desired picture, you will discover this instruction with another figure. Repetitions could thus be avoided.

Having a good command of different basic techniques surely is the basis for a successful and original looking chocolate figure. This good command, however, is preceded by practice, practice, practice. I wish you a lot of patience and pleasure.

# 1. How to Use Couvertures

## 1.1 Different Melting Methods

### Chopping of Couvertures
The melting process can be accelerated by dissolving the chopped couverture. Use a clean, dry and odourless chopping board!

### Melting in the Tempering Apparatus
The couverture can also be melted in the tempering apparatus or in a warming cupboard. These devices should produce an absolutely dry heat, without any ventilation to avoid encrustation.

### Dissolving in the Bain-Marie
Be careful! The water must not boil to avoid the generation of steam (water temperature 60 °C / 140 °F). The bowl should exactly fit in the bain-marie (it should not swim).

### Dissolving in the Micro-Wave Oven
Small amounts up to approx. 3 kgs / 6.6 lbs. can be melted in the micro-wave oven. Chop the couverture, the finer the better. Work in several intervals. Stir well after each interval. Control the temperature during the entire process. Do not leave the wooden spoon in the container during melting process.

## 1.2 Tempering the Couverture

**Traditional Tempering**

Two thirds of the couverture melted at 45 to 50 °C / 113 to 122 °F should be allowed to cool down on the marble table. Spread and scrape together with a spatula until you have obtained a thick consistency.

Mix the cold tempered couverture with the warm couverture and stir well (do not beat!). The temperature should now be 28 °C / 82.4 °F. Now warm the couverture carefully up to the working temperature (32 °C / 89 °F).

### Traditional Tempering Method

45° to 50 °C / 113 to 122 °F    Melting range

Processing temperatures:
30 to 33 °C / 86 to 91.4 °F    Dark couverture
30 to 32 °C / 86 to 89.6 °F    Milk couverture
30 to 32 °C / 86 to 89.6 °F    White couverture

20 °C / 68 °F    Room temperature
18 °C / 64.4 °F    Storage temperature

### Vaccination or "Seeding" Method

Mix one third grated couverture with two thirds melted couverture (45 to 50 °C / 113 to 122 °F) and stir well. Depending on the temperature, add more or less of the grated couverture.

The processing temperature of 30 to 32 °C / 86 to 89.6 °F can be reached by slightly re-warming the mixture or by adding warm couverture.

### Vaccination or "Seeding" Method:

45 to 50 °C / 113 to 122 °F    Melting range

Processing Temperatures:
30 to 33 °C / 86 to 91.4 °F    Dark couverture
30 to 32 °C / 86 to 89.6 °F    Milk couverture
30 to 32 °C / 86 to 89.6 °F    White couverture

20 °C / 68 °F    Room temperature
18 °C / 64.4 °F    Storage temperature

If the couverture cools down too much during tempering or vaccination, the correct consistency cannot be reached anymore by warming it up again. The couverture is thick and can only be corrected by remelting (45 to 50 °C / 113 to 122 °F) and temper again.

### Direct Warm-Up Method

#### Warming Up in the Micro-Wave Oven
Finely chop couverture. Melt couverture at intervals of approx. 30 seconds and stir well in-between. Note: Consider the heat compensation towards the end of the melting process, i.e. let it sit for a moment, stir well and control the temperature! Processing temperature: 30 to 32 °C / 86 to 89.6 °F.

#### Warming Up in the Tempering Apparatus
Fill the tempering apparatus with the coarsely chopped couverture in the evening and set the thermostat. Stir well the next morning. Processing temperature: 30 to 32 °C / 86 to 89.6 °F. Setting the thermostat (35 to 38 °C / 95 to 100.4 °F) will require some practice at first until time and quantity data comply (therefore, better set a deeper temperature and warm up the couverture if necessary).

### Direct Method:

Processing Temperatures:
30 to 33 °C / 86 to 91.4 °F    Dark couverture
30 to 32 °C / 86 to 89.6 °F    Milk couverture
30 to 32 °C / 86 to 89.6 °F    White couverture

20 °C / 68 °F    Room temperature
18 °C / 64.4 °F    Storage temperature

Increasing the processing temperature of the couverture by more than 0.5 °C will destroy the homogenous structure of the cocoa butter and the tempering process will have to be repeated. Melt totally (45 to 50 °C / 113 to 122 °F) and temper.

# 1.4 Important Tips for Processing and Storage

* Melting temperature of couverture: not more than 50 °C / 122 °F. Especially milk couvertures and white couvertures.

* Avoid any contact with steam during melting process. Ideal water temperature 60 °C / 140 °F.

* Mix the couverture well after melting. Do no beat the couverture since otherwise it will become frothy!

* Workroom temperature: approx. 20 °C / 66 to 68 °F.

* The filling of the chocolates to be coated with couverture should have room temperature.

* If you keep the couverture in a liquid consistency for several days, the solid matters and the cocoa butter will separate. So either stir two or three times a day or allow to solidify after use.

* Close well opened packages.

* Couverture, especially grated couverture, easily absorbs humidity and becomes sandy. In this case it is no longer possible to completely dissolve the couverture.

* Couverture is very delicate as regards taste. Under no circumstances store couverture with strong smelling food products.

* White couverture, moreover, is sensitive to light.

* Do not store cast Easter articles in the cellar, which is exclusively lighted by artificial light. Even neon light has a negative effect on the quality of the couverture.

* In most cases vegetable fats and couverture do not harmonise and have a negative effect on the gloss. The so-called "fat bloom" will be generated.

## The Couverture is Too Thick:

* Water vapour inclusions: Melting the couverture in the bain-marie bears the risk of water vapour inclusion. In countries with high atmospheric humidity this risk is permanently inherent. Influences by water and water vapour can normally not be corrected. Such couverture can only be used for fillings and sauces. As a remedy: Cover chromium-steel utensils with aluminium foil, no matter whether the couverture is in a solid or in a dissolved state.

* Moist board for grating: Always use dry boards.

* Opened packages had not been thoroughly closed:
Especially the packages of couverture drops have to be closed thoroughly. Drops have a by far larger surface than a couverture block. For that reason a larger amount of humidity can deposit.

* Couverture cooled down too much during the tempering: If the couverture cools down too much, a large amount of stable cocoa butter crystals will develop. Since cocoa butter crystals multiply, the couverture becomes thick. For that reason the exact temperatures have to be stuck to during tempering.

* You left the warmed couverture untouched for a too long period without using it: In a permanently moved, tempered couverture the cocoa butter crystals do multiply less quick than in a couverture that has been left untouched. If the couverture develops a skin with a greasy consistency, carefully stir and slightly warm up this couverture. The crystal structure of the cocoa butter will quickly dissolve and the couverture will liquefy. This process has to be carried through with extreme conscientiousness and the temperature has to be controlled permanently.

Repeat tempering process:
Melt to 45 to 50 °C / 113 to 122 °F, then temper again.

# 2. Moulding of Hollow Forms

The conventional metal and plastic forms are widespread and are also the best for this purpose. To encounter no problems during moulding, the forms have to be correctly treated and prepared. It is surprising how many articles of daily life can be used for the production.

**Some Tips:**

* Never scrape off the couverture parts from the form with a hard object such as e.g. a knife or spatula. The durability of the forms depends upon this treatment.

* Wash the forms with warm soap water and give it a good rinse afterwards.

* Dry with a soft piece of cloth.

* Wipe the interior surface of the forms with clean cotton prior to filling.

* The forms should have room temperature for moulding.

In the case of forms with many details it may be of advantage to brush them first. This will avoid the formation of bubbles.

If you want the hollow bodies to show an extraordinary gloss, spray the forms with thinned couverture first and then pour in the couverture. This method also allows to create shades with couvertures of different colours.

Fill the forms until the couverture shows the desired thickness. Thin-walled hollow bodies can be obtained by beating the rim of the form with a rolling pin or a rubber club while the couverture is running out.

Put the forms on a wire-rack for draining. In the case of two-piece forms, which will be stuck after moulding, a small couverture deposit at the edge of the forms is desirable.

As soon as the couverture begins to harden, remove the forms from the wire-rack and put into the refrigerator until the couverture comes completely off the form.

Don't fill again until the form has room temperature.

Never put moulded forms into the deep freezer for cooling. During moulding a film of condensed water will develop in the form. This film hinders the gloss and you will be confronted with problems when moulding again.

# 3. Pouring of Flat Surfaces

Flat surfaces can be obtained by working against the natural contraction of the couverture on the silicone paper using some tricks. Below you can find three suitable methods:

1. Evenly spread the couverture on the silicone paper or silicone mat. As soon as the couverture begins to harden, turn the couverture plate and loosen the paper. Now you have got a few minutes to cut out decorations without any problems.

2. Evenly spread the couverture on the silicone paper or silicone mat. Allow to harden a bit. Spread a second layer of couverture and cover the liquid couverture with a piece of silicone paper immediately. To avoid air bubbles, smooth out with the flat of the hand. You'd best use a painter's roll.

If the couverture plate is put onto a wooden board, you've got more time for further treatment (wood is warmer than chromium steel or marble).

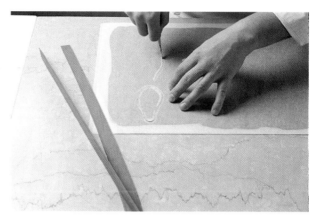

Turn the couverture plate and cut out the desired form through the paper at once. The ideal cutting knife has a thin short blade, which allows to evenly cut out details without any problems.

By spreading two layers of couverture and applying silicone paper on the bottom and the top, the couverture will not contract: The couverture surface will not bend.

3. Slightly oil the surfaces selected (e.g. chromium steel table) and put on a plastic sheeth. Smooth out the air bubbles with a scraper. Evenly spread the couverture on the plastic sheet. The plastic and the couverture virtually stick to the surface and cannot bend.

This method is especially suitable for the production of cut-out decoration elements, which are to receive a fine gloss. This kind of decoration design is mostly applied in pastry and fancy cake production.

# 4. Moulding of Pipes and Sticks

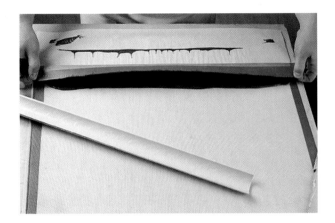

There are two methods to make pipes:

1. Spread the couverture on a silicone paper or mat to the desired width. The larger the pipe diameter the more solid the material on which you spread the couverture. For thick walls spread a layer of couverture and allow to set a bit. Then spread the second layer of couverture and overlap the long side of the couverture band to the other long side. Join the two edges and roll in such a manner as to form a pipe.

If you want to cut the couverture pipe to size later, it should not completely crystallise. This means that you should take it out of the refrigerator after 3 or 5 minutes. Loosen the silicone mat and immediately cut off the desired length from the pipe.

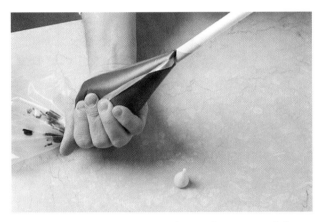

2. Roll thin pipes using wooden rods. Many of these thin pipes will be completely filled.

To avoid air bubbles in the filling, fill the pipes with the piping bag from the bottom. The pipes are closed with a marzipan plug to prevent the couverture from running out.

# 5. Sketching of Ideas

Transfer the outlines of all moulds to a cardboard and cut out. Now you can begin to sketch. What a surprise! Is it really that simple to sketch ideas?

You should make it your habit to begin to sketch as soon as you want to convert an idea or when you work on a special order. Thus you will always know exactly how the finished figure has to look like and you can also work quicker.

The collection and sketching of ideas is a never-ending process. In your everyday life you do encounter situations and object, which may be the idea for an ingenious design. Now it is necessary to fix these ideas. A note pad or a camera are useful items when you go for a walk etc. and finally these ideas can be made "suitable for couverture" by means of cardboard stencils.

# 6. Stencilling Technique

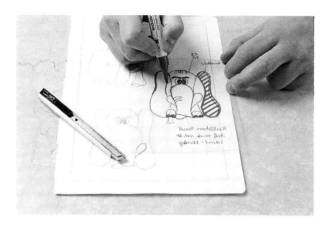

This elephant is a self-made sketch and shows how simple it is to sketch your own creations with the aid of cardboard stencils.

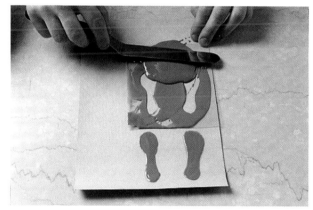

Normally you would cut the ears out of the couverture or model them. Cutting out and modelling are very good techniques, which, however, take some more time than the stencilling technique.

The stencilling technique allows to produce difficult flat single components in a short time. The motif is drawn onto a plastic foil, which is stable but flexible enough. Then take a carpet knife to cut out the motif and the stencil is ready and can be covered with couverture.

If you want to produce bent decoration elements, put the spread elements in a pastry form or over a corrugated sheet.

# 7. Sticking Together of Figures

Put a tray on a pan with boiling water. To join two cast shells, melt the edges on the warm tray and put the two shells together afterwards.

The edges of couverture bodies can be melted on warm metal forms, so they will fit closer to the basic form.

Remove the melted couverture at the join with your fingers. This saves having to remove hardened couverture later.

Unevenness of showpieces can be levelled with over-crystallised, too thick couverture. Clean such spots after hardening, so they are no longer visible.

This method of correcting uneven spots with thickened couverture is not recommendable for series products, since this method is rather time-consuming.

It partly takes a very long time until the melted couverture hardens at the joins and thus fixes two parts. This process can be considerable shortened by spraying a cold spray directly onto the join.

# 8. Making Moulds

Silicone or wax moulds are best suited to manufacture large series. They help to save time and to simplify detail work.

## One-Piece Mould (Reliefs)

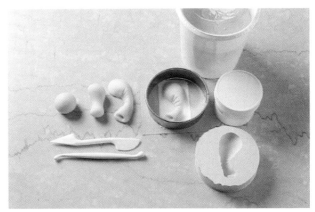

Put the original of the relief into a correspondingly high container. Allow 2 or 3 cm / 0.78 × 1.18 in. for the form edge. Firmly fix the form to the bottom of the container with double tape to avoid floating up of the part to copy. If the model does not fit firmly to the bottom, holes and gaps will be filled.

## Two-Piece Mould (Silicone Form)

Put the model into a container and embed in Plasticine. Take care that the bottom of the original fits close to the containers' edge (opening to pour in). Press some holes into the Plasticine, which will later avoid that the two old parts will dislocate each other.

The visible surface of the original and the Plasticine should be brushed with a separating agent.

Mix silicone with hardener and fill into the mould. Allow the silicone mixture to harden. Turn over, remove the Plasticine and brush the surface of the original and of the silicone mould with a separating agent and fill with silicone again.

Let the silicone harden. Take out the original and then put together the silicone mould.

These moulds can be used the same way as normal casting moulds.

## Gelatine Moulds

Bring 600 g / 21 oz. water to boil, add 100 g / 3.5 oz. powdered gelatine and mix with the whisk.

As soon as the gelatine has dissolved and the mixture begins to become transparent, remove from the heat (gelatine should never boil!).

Dip the bottom of the mould to be cast into the gelatine and then stick the original mould into the middle of a casting mould.

Put the mould into the deep-freezer for approx. 3 minutes.

The gelatine should have 45 °C / 113 °F and should be liquid; pour the gelatine over the cool mould. All ends of the mould (5 to 10 cm / 1.9 to 3.9 inches) should have an adequate edge.

Cool for some hours.

Cut the gelatine into two or more pieces with a sharp knife and carefully take out the original. Put together the gelatine mould again and fasten with some rubber bands or an adhesive tape.

Prior to filling the mould, cool it down to 3 to 6 °C / 37.4 to 42.8 °F. Fill like any other mould.

Store the gelatine mixture in the refrigerator or the deep-freezer, because otherwise blue mould will form at once. Melt in the microwave oven, because there isn't hardly any risk to burn the gelatine mixture. For large figures fill in the gelatine in several

layers and cool each layer separately, since otherwise the buoyancy force will make the figure swim.

## Forms of Band-Iron

Sketch the outline of the figure to be cut out. Draw the different spaces onto the band-iron. Bend the band-iron according to the model and fix at the ends.

## Latex Forms

The stabilised, liquid latex modelling material, which is based on natural rubber concentrate, can be used for the production of seamless hose forms. This pre-vulcanised latex is ready-for-use and hardens in the open air without addition of a hardener.

Nearly all figures, sculptures and many other objects can be made of latex. For this purpose brush the latex several times (eight to ten times, depending on the size of the original) onto the model. You can also dip the original figure into the liquid latex. The modelling material will then harden in the open air and will form a solid form skin.

After complete hardening the form skin is peeled off the original model and used to mould a number of second models.

# 9. Spraying Techniques

The spray gun with a compressor (the pressure is 3 to 5 atmospheres above atmospheric pressure) and the handy electric sprayer are the two best-known devices to spray couverture. It is recommended to warm up these two implements in the warming cupboard prior to use.

Add a sufficient amount of liquid cocoa butter (approx. 30 to 50 %) to the warm couverture, so that the couverture shows an oily consistency. The more cocoa butter you add, the finer the structure. Thus the couverture is warmed up by some more degrees than normal, but is then cooled down by the compressed air. This will produce a fine gloss on the chocolate figure.

The figures are put into a self-made spraying chamber or a vapour-free, cool dishwasher.

The first layer will be applied from a distance of approx. 40 cm / 17,7 in. Take care not to apply a too thick layer of chocolate, since otherwise unsightly drops will form! Spraying will not conceal faults, on the contrary, slightly uneven spots and bubbles will be even more conspicuous. Such faults can be eliminated before the second layer is spread.

To breathe life into a figure, the shading is sprayed with couverture of a different colour.

Ideal temperatures:
Room temperature        20 °C / 68 °F
Chocolate figure         20 °C / 68 °F
Couverture temperature 33 to 34 °C / 91.4 to 93.2 °F

## Spraying on Deep-Frozen Bodies

Changes in colour and structure can be obtained with the following trick: Put the figures into the deep-freezer for 15 to 20 minutes. The deep-frozen figures are immediately sprayed, with the couverture particles forming crystals in the same moment when they hit the figure, which will give the figure a velvety appearance. Do not touch the figure until the condensed water has completely evaporated. Due to the rough surface it is possible to apply food colours with the airbrush to create shades.

If you put the figure in the refrigerator for 30 to 40 minutes, you can obtain a similar effect. You should also use tempered couverture for spraying, because if you use untempered couverture to spray thick coatings, you run the risk that the chocolate will not crystallise the way you want.

# 10. Modelling with Couverture

Although the consistency of modelling couverture is firmer than marzipan, the modelling technique is the same. This method is described in various books in detail.

The modelling couverture is used for parts, which cannot be produced with pure couverture or wherever cutting out of couverture is too intricate.

Modelling couverture is also used instead of marzipan, because it increases the stability of the figure and doesn't dry out so fast.

Modelling couverture for series products should be of best quality. The material should not be called plastic chocolate, because this will not be beneficial to the sale of the products.

## Recipes for Modelling Couverture

### Dark Modelling Couverture
| | |
|---|---|
| 1000 g / 35.3 oz | dark couverture |
| 300 g / 10.6 oz. | glucose |
| 200 g / 7 oz. | syrup 30 ° Bé |

### Brown Modelling Couverture
| | |
|---|---|
| 1200 g / 42.36 oz. | milk couverture |
| 300 g / 10.6 oz | glucose |
| 200 g / 7 oz. | syrup 30 ° Bé |

### White or Coloured Modelling Couverture
| | |
|---|---|
| 1500 g / 52.95 oz. | white icing |
| 150 g / 5.3 oz | sugar |
| 600 g / 21.2 oz. | glucose |
| 200 g / 7 oz. | syrup 30 ° Bé |

**Preparation and Processing**

* Warm the glucose to 40 °C / 104 °F. If you want a coloured modelling couverture, add the colour now.

* Add all other ingredients (except couverture) and mix well.

* Add tempered couverture and mix well again.

* Pour onto a marble slab and let harden.

* Store in an air-tight container.

* Let through a roller several times prior to use to make the modelling couverture supple or slightly warm in the microwave oven.

* Roll out the modelling couverture between plastic foils (thus you will not produce the white spots on the surface caused by the powdered sugar).

* Rub the surface of the modelling couverture with the inner sides of your hands (this will give a beautiful gloss).

# 11. Eyes

The eyes are the most important part of all figures in this book. As is the case with people, the first thing you look at are the eyes of the figures. If the eyes are lively, if they twinkle with fun or charm, you will like the figure at once. No matter how perfect the figure may be, without expression on its face, it won't attract the customer.

The pupils will scarcely ever be piped into the middle of the eye, with the cowboy, who has just been shot into his back perhaps being the exception. This would cause this vacant look.

If the pupils are placed to the edge of the eye, the eyes become lively, no matter, whether they squint or look to the right, the left or the top. Just try!

## Four Ways to Form the Eyes

Pipe dark couverture spots into small egg forms or half balls. While doing so, put the forms at an angle. Pupils in the middle of the eyes will cause a glassy stare without life and charm.

For a three-colour eye pipe some milk chocolate into the form before you fill the form with white couverture.

Self-rolled piping bags are ideal for piping pupils, because the amount of couverture can be dosed better with the opening of this piping bag. Piping bags of plastic are less suited for this purpose, since they are a bit clumsy for such a precise work.

Warm an oval praline cutter over a flame and melt out the eyes.
Place truffle shells into the egg form from behind and fix with couverture.

Mark the parts to be melted out and melt out with the hot point of a knife.

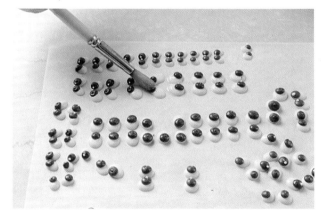

Pipe white couverture spots onto silicone paper and immediately pipe dark couverture pupils onto the eyes. As soon as the couverture eyes are hard, brush them with nougat or marzipan varnish. This will isolate the couverture and will on the one hand prevent unsightly finger prints, on the other hand the eyes will have an extraordinary gloss.

# 12. Silk Screen Printing Process

The silk screen printing process has been used in the graphic industry for a long time. This technique more and more makes its entry into the confectionery trade.

Copy the motifs selected onto a transparent foil. The silk screen studio will then transfer this copy onto a screen and put it on a frame. The production of the frame and of the screen is rather expensive, however, the screen can be exposed again and again, which is rather favourable.

Now liquid cocoa, cocoa paste or pre-fabricated writing chocolate is pressed through the screen. This is either made on marzipan, modelling couverture or simply on a piece of plastic, which will later be covered with couverture.

If you want a coloured print, bleach white couverture or cocoa butter with approx. 2 or 5 % titanium oxide (white colour). Now mix the white couverture with oil-soluble powdery colours. The coloured mass must be very bright, since otherwise you will hardly be able to make out the print.

This method offers a lot of space for individual customer service. An old class photo, funny congratulatory cards or firms' logos are made very quickly.

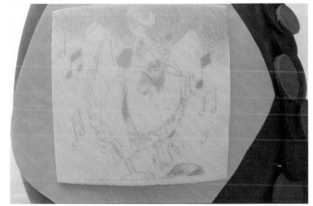

Large, extravagantly decorated Easter eggs are an Italian tradition, this egg is a modern version.

# 13. Cocoa Painting

A kind of decoration, which is used very seldom. It is best suited for showpieces.

You need light and firm marzipan. Roll to 3 mm / 0.11 in. and let dry.

Cover the desired motif with wax paper or silicone paper and trace the contours with a soft pencil laterally inverted. Put the reverse side of the paper onto the marzipan and trace the contours with a pencil again.

## Cocoa for Painting

Either melted block cocoa, mixed with vegetable oil (more or less, depending on the desired intensity of the colour), or pre-fabricated cocoa paste, mixed with oil (more or less, depending on the desired intensity of the colour).

## Brush

A very fine quality paintbrush is ideal, because you have the possibility to paint all details. A thicker brush, in turn, is better suited for priming.

## Protection

As soon as the painting is dry, spray the picture with nougat varnish. Never use a brush for sealing, because you might smear the painting! Such a picture can be preserved for many years in a dust-free surrounding.

## Technique

For this figure the picture was primed with a very light cocoa colour first. This means that the cocoa was mixed with plenty of oil.

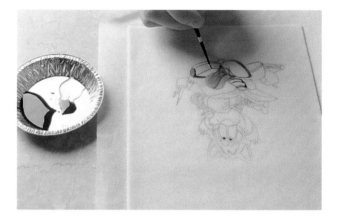

Note: Faults can be eliminated better on a light priming coat; it can therefore not be recommended in all cases to work with very dark shades right from the beginning.

Now you can continuously use richer shades. Colour nuances should be flowing, because this will give the figures a lifelike touch.

The richest black shades are applied with undiluted cocoa paste.

This technique may be the most difficult method, but it is the most impressive one. A more simple way is to fill the single parts of the figure with undiluted cocoa paste, to leave some parts white and to use diluted cocoa paste for some other parts. Thus you can obtain intense contrasts in colour.

The first more difficult procedure strikes out the artistic aspect, whereas the latter emphasises more the handicraft character due to the strict proceeding according to the pattern.

The teacher again gave me lines.
Now I have to write 100 times "I must not eat an apple during the lesson".

# SERIES PRODUCTS

The main season for such chocolate figures certainly is the cold season, around occasions like Easter, Christmas or Valentine's Day. But if you give free rein to your imagination, you will find motifs for all seasons that can be made of chocolate. Original chocolate caricatures are excellently suited as gifts, which will give great pleasure to the recipient of the gift. Within a short time, the confectionery business will build up a reputation due to the funny creations and the image as a specialised business will increase.

With some practice you will manage the work routine in an instant. In the same way the love for the profession will grow with your employees, because creativity probably is the most beautiful aspect of this profession.

Body:       Couverture shell, Ø = 5 cm / 1.97 in.
Head:       Couverture shell, Ø = 5 cm / 1.97 in.
Feet:       Couverture egg,
            4.5 x 2.6 cm / 1.77 x 1.02 in.
Ears:       Couverture half-shell, Ø = 4.2 cm / 1.65 in.
Muzzle:     Couverture half-shell, Ø = 2.5 cm / 0.98 in.
Cheese:     Marzipan, 5 mm/0,19 in. thick,
            heart-shaped pastry cutter

Minor details make the difference. The heart becomes a more vital appearance, if it is cut out through a plastic foil. Without doing so, it would have an angular effect and would not look as real.

After cutting out, the marzipan is coloured with an airbrush. Thus you need less food colour and you can obtain a more lively effect. The shading thus produced will even increase this effect.

"I can't stand it any longer. I have been smelling this Emmental Cheese for ages, but I am not allowed to bite into it."

# HOLY SANTA CLAUS

Body:       Couverture, cast champagne glass
Shoes:      Couverture half-shell, Ø = 2.5 cm / 0.98 in.
Whiskers and
goatee:     Marzipan, Ø = 12.5 cm / 4.92 in.,
            grooved, 2 mm / 0.08 in. thick
Hands:      Marzipan, 10 g / 0.35 oz. each
Nose:       Marzipan, 2.5 g / 0.08 oz.
Mouth:      Marzipan
Moustache:  Marzipan, Ø = 4 cm / 1.57 in.,
            2 mm/0.08 in. thick
Brim of hat: Marzipan, rolled out to a thickness
            of 5 mm / 0.19 in., 1 cm / 0.39 in. wide,
            cut out through plastic foil
Tip of hat:  Marzipan or truffle shell
Weight:     95 g / 3.35 oz.

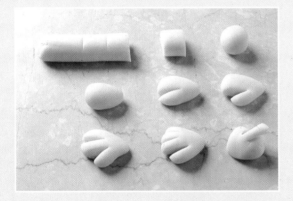 

Modelling marzipan is the material for the hands. As is the case with almost all modelled parts, you have to roll a ball first. After you have formed a drop, groove in the thumb of Santa Claus and slightly press together. The exhortatory finger is the most important part of this figure and is therefore emphasised.

For the brim of the hat cut the marzipan into strips through a plastic foil and immediately press one side into refined sugar in crystals. The sugar will stick to the soft marzipan. As soon as the marzipan begins to dry, the sugar will no longer stick to the marzipan this way.

"The marzipan sticks pretty well to my face.
I can hardly wait to get rid of this beard and that the Christmas commotion will finally be over."

Boots:           Couverture, moulded champagne glass,
                 stuck together with a couverture egg,
                 10 x 6.7 cm / 3.9 x 2.6 in.
Sole of
the boots:       Modelling couverture, 3 mm / 0.1 in. thick,
                 26 cm / 10.23 in. long, 1 cm / 0.39 in. wide,
Head:            Couverture shell, Ø = 6 cm / 2.36 in.
Ears:            Truffle shell, stuck together
Muzzle:          2 couverture eggs,
                 each 4.4 x 2.6 cm / 1.73 x 1.02 in.
Cap:             Marzipan, 3 mm / 0.11 in. thick
Brim
of cap:          Marzipan roll, pressed into refined sugar
                 in crystals
Tassel:          Marzipan
Boot top:        Marzipan roll, pressed into refined sugar
                 in crystals, 1 cm / 0.39 in. wide,
                 5 mm / 0.19 in. thick
Gloves:          Marzipan, 10 g / 0.35 oz.
Weight:          190 g / 6.7 oz.

The muzzle of the bear is a bit difficult and time-consuming, which is, however, justified by the achieved effect. You can also use pre-fabricated egg-shaped hollow forms, which are normally used for the production of pralines. This will save some time.

The cap (15 x 6 x 6 cm / 5.9 x 2.36 x 2.36 in.) is formed last and is fit directly to the head of the bear. Press the brim and the tassel into refined sugar crystals and fix to the cap using some egg white.

"It's not fair. People put us in their smelly boots and really think we would enjoy it."

# ANGEL

Body:     Couverture, moulded shell
Head:     Couverture shell, Ø = 4.2 cm / 1.65 in.
Hair:     Marzipan, Ø = 4.2 cm / 1.65 in.
Hands:    Marzipan, 4 g / 0.14 oz. each
Candle:   Marzipan, 5 g / 0.17 oz.
Wick:     Chopped almonds
Weight:   120 g / 4.23 oz.

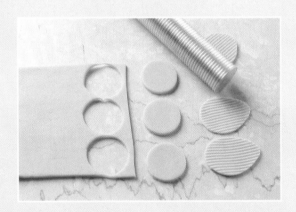

The marzipan for the hair should be rolled last, so it is still smooth. By grooving the marzipan after cutting out, the hair becomes an individual and natural look.

Take care that the head is not too big, because otherwise you won't see the base of the wings (where the shell gets smaller) and the figure loses some of its elegance.

An angel formed of shells attracted the author's attention on the occasion of a Sunday walk with friends in Newport, Rhode Island. He at once pulled out his note pad and captured it on paper.

# BUNNY COOL

Body:     Couverture, moulded white wine glass
Head:     Couverture shell, Ø = 6 cm / 2.36 in.
Ears:     Couverture, shape of a ship
Glasses:  Couverture, stencilled with chocolate
          cover foil
Muzzle:   Couverture half-shell, Ø = 2.5 cm / 0.98 in.
Teeth:    White decoration mass
Coat:     Modelling couverture
Hair:     Modelling couverture
Hand:     Modelling couverture
Weight:   185 g / 6.53 oz.

The cool glasses are made by using a praline cover foil. The two glasses of the spectacles are stuck together with some couverture.

The beautiful hairdo supports the wild look: press soft modelling couverture through the garlic press and fix immediately.

"Don't tell me again that you're only checking out where the wind is coming from!"

| | |
|---|---|
| Top hat: | Couverture, moulded yoghurt glass |
| Head: | Couverture shell, Ø = 6 cm / 2.36 in. |
| Ears: | Couverture, stencilled |
| Cheeks: | Couverture egg, 4.2 x 2.7 cm / 1.65 x 1.06 in., and couverture shell, Ø = 2.2 cm / 0.86 in. |
| Nose: | Couverture egg, 4.2 x 2.7 cm / 1.65 x 1.06 in. |
| Hair: | Marzipan, pressed through a sieve |
| Weight: | 155 g / 5.47 oz. |

These ears give the bunnies an elegant appearance. The spread ears are put into a form as long as the couverture is still smooth. Due to this self-made stencil, the production of the ears does not take much time.

The hair is pressed through a sieve. Different mesh densities will produce varying effects.

"How did the reproduction of rabbits work again? They didn't mention anything about the trick with the hat in sex education class. Or, maybe, I slept through that part."

| Body: | Couverture egg, |
| --- | --- |
| | 8.3 x 5.4 cm / 3.26 x 2.12 in. |
| Head: | Couverture shell, Ø = 6 cm / 2.36 in. |
| Hands: | Marzipan, 12 g / 0.42 oz. |
| Feet: | Couverture egg, 6.2 x 3.8 cm / 2.44 x 1.5 in. |
| Teeth: | Couverture |
| Nose: | Modelling couverture, 5 g / 0.17 oz. |
| Cheeks: | Marzipan, 5 g / 0.17 oz. each |
| Ears: | Marzipan, cut out |
| Glasses: | Couverture, stencilled with praline cover foil |
| Thighs: | Couverture egg, |
| | 4.5 x 2.6 cm / 1.77 x 1.02 in. |
| Hat: | Bought plaited hat |
| Weight: | 170 g / 6 oz. |

The plaited hat completes the funny appearance. You can buy such a hat in a decoration shop for only a small amount of money.

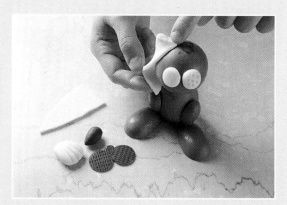

A bunny with hanging ears is something quite different. When packing the figure, these ears do not fall off quite so easy. For a pair of ears you only need one stencil. Divide the ears into two immediately after cutting and fix them to the head.

James Bunny 007 – "License to eat"
"What do you think, shall we eat a cabbage? Or are these cabbages counted?"
"We will only eat them as soon as the confectioner averts his eyes."

# CHICKEN

| | |
|---|---|
| Body: | Couverture egg,<br>10 x 6.7 cm / 3.93 x 2.36 in. |
| Wings: | Couverture, cut out |
| Comb: | Marzipan, 5 drops, 4 g / 0.14 oz. each |
| Beak: | Marzipan, 7 g / 0.24 oz. |
| Eye lid: | Couverture egg,<br>4.3 x 2.7 cm / 1.69 x 1.06 in. |
| Weight: | 150 g / 5.29 oz. |

This chicken has an extremely simple structure but nevertheless it is very expressive. Since in this case the customer's attention is attracted by very few details, these details should be worked very precisely.

To have more time for working, the couverture plate is put onto a wooden board. The wings are cut out with the aid of stencils.

"The author couldn't think of a silly saying on my figure. I am just boringly normal.
But after all, I am quickly manufactured."

# WALRUS

| | |
|---|---|
| Body: | Couverture egg, 10 x 6.7 cm / 3.93 x 2.36 in. |
| Muzzle: | Couverture egg, 4.3 x 2.7cm / 1.69 x 1.06 in. |
| Eye brows: | Modelling couverture |
| Tusks: | Modelling couverture |
| Nose: | Modelling couverture |
| Front fin: | Modelling couverture |
| Tail fin: | Modelling couverture |
| Weight: | 160 g / 5.64 oz. |

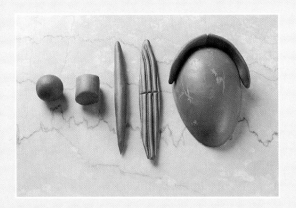

The oblong roll of modelling couverture is marked with a grooved rolling pin. The marked eyebrows give the walrus an aged expression.

The fins are cut out through plastic foil. The disc is cut in two.

"The peddler really tried to sell denture fixative to us.
But these are still our first teeth."

# BLUES SISTERS

| | |
|---|---|
| Body: | Couverture egg, 6.2 x 3.8 cm / 2.44 x 1.5 in. |
| Head: | Couverture shell, Ø = 4.2 cm / 1.65 in. |
| Wings: | Couverture, stencilled |
| Beak: | Marzipan |
| Flippers: | Marzipan, pressed into a wax mould |
| Hair: | Marzipan, pressed through a garlic press |
| Tongue: | Marzipan |
| Glasses: | Couverture, stencilled |
| Weight: | 85 g / 3 oz. |

The beak is made first. It keeps its form, if you allow the marzipan to dry a bit. Fold together the marzipan and immediately press against the wall of a pastry cutter. Due to the larger contact surface it is easier to fasten the beak.

Since the wings and the glasses can be made with stencils and the flippers with a wax mould, the cost calculation of this figure is very interesting.

These figures reminded the author very much of the Blues brothers. Cool glasses and a big mouth.

# SITTING BUNNY

Body: See opposite recipe
Head: Couverture shell, Ø = 6 cm / 2.36 in.
Muzzle: Marzipan disk
Ears: Couverture, separately piped
Hair: Combed couverture drop
Tail: Couverture egg, 3.1 x 2.2 cm / 0.86 in.
3.1 x 2.2 cm / 1.22 x 0.86 in.

**Recipe for Bunny Body Filling**
200 g / 7.06 oz. rice crispies
100 g / 3.53 oz. dried apricot dices
100 g / 3.53 oz. raisins
100 g / 3.53 oz. date dices
600 g / 21.18 oz. milk couverture
100 g / 3.53 oz. cocoa butter, liquid

Mix all ingredients and use a spoon to fill the mixture into the form.

Pipe the ears with thickened couverture. Let harden and cut off the end of the couverture drop. Join both ears with couverture.

The problem with this bunny is that he has such a tasty body.
Therefore he is immediately eaten after a quick look.

# BIRD IN THE NEST

| | |
|---|---|
| Body: | Couverture egg, 6.2 x 3.8 cm / 2.44 x 1.5 in. |
| Head: | Couverture shell, Ø = 4.2 cm / 1.65 in. |
| Nest: | Couverture, moulded savarin form |
| Wings: | Couverture egg, 4.5 x 2.6 cm / 1.77 x 1.02 in. |
| Tail feathers: | Modelling couverture, 6 x 3 x 2 cm / 2.36 x 1.18 x 0.78 in., 2 mm / 0.08 in. thick |
| Hair: | Modelling marzipan, pressed through a garlic press |
| Beak: | Marzipan, 1 g / 0.035 oz. |
| Weight: | 120 g / 4.23 oz. |

Brush a savarin ring of couverture with untempered couverture and roll in roasted chopped almonds. Thoroughly spray with couverture afterwards.

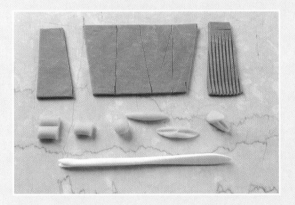

The beak of this bird must be small and pointed. Thus it differs from a duck or other birds. The figure is given some elegance by the tail of modelling couverture. First the tail is cut and then it is grooved.

"How long are we still supposed to pipe our beaks hoarse?" –
"Patience, Mum will soon return with some fat insects."

# BIRTHDAY FIGURES

Figure:    Couverture, cut with stencil
Nose:      Marzipan
Teeth:     Modelling couverture

The simplest decoration certainly is the birthday decoration for a child. Any original animal made of marzipan and a few candles will come up to the expectations of most children. But what are we to decorate, if we have no information about the profession, the hobbies or other predilections of an adult? The author faced this problem so many times in the past. A bought, pre-fabricated marzipan label is incompatible with ones professional honour and to use flowers as decoration for the thousandst time is not what you want. With these figures you can always offer an attractive and humorous decoration.

First you have to manufacture the stencils for the figures. The stencils are put onto the spread couverture plate and the figures are then cut out along the border of the stencils. These figures are excellently suited for storage and you are always prepared for unexpected orders.

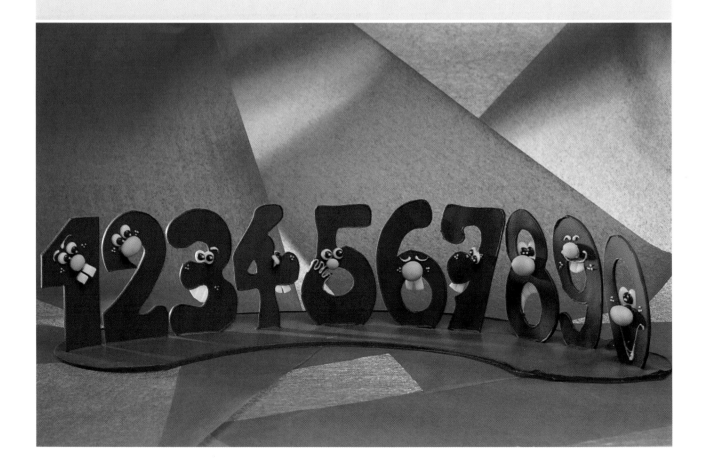

Which decoration is best suited for a birthday cake for a seventeen-year-old?

# WHALE

| | |
|---|---|
| Body: | Couverture egg, 10 x 6.7 cm / 3.93 x 2.36 in. |
| Tail fin: | Couverture, stencilled |
| Teeth: | White marzipan, 3 mm / 0.11 in. thick, grooved with a grooving pin |
| Lip: | Modelling couverture |
| Wave: | Couverture, brushed onto a corrugated sheet of plastic |
| Weight: | 155 g / 5.47 oz. |

The tail fin gives the whale a lively look and elegance. For that reason it is of utmost importance to put the stencilled fin into a half-round baking tin at once.

Roof covering of corrugated plastic for the production of an ocean wave can be bought in garden centres. It is important to brush the plastic until the couverture layer has the desired thickness. As long as the couverture has not fully crystallised, you can cut the desired size of the wave with a stencil. Let harden in the refrigerator.

One sales promotion measure could e.g. be to donate a certain amount of the selling price of each whale to WWF or Greenpeace. An attempt that will surely pay dividends.

Body:       Couverture, cut out
Head:       Couverture half-shell, Ø = 6 cm / 2.36 in.
Muzzle:     Couverture egg,
            4.3 x 2.7 cm / 1.69 x 1.06 in.
Nose:       Modelling couverture, 5 g / 0.17 oz.
Horns:      Modelling couverture, 3 g / 0.1 oz. each
Ears:       Couverture egg,
            3.1 x 2.1 cm / 1.22 x 0.82 in.
Hind leg:   Couverture, stencilled
Tail:       Marzipan, 6 g / 0.21 oz
Grass:      Thickened couverture, piped
Weight:     140 g / 4.9 oz.

The hind and fore legs are stencilled. In contrast to most of the other figures, you only need a half-shell for the head of these cows.

Thickened couverture: thicken tempered couverture with some drops of water. Advantage: piped ornaments are thicker and thus more stable. In this case the individual leaves of grass become clearly visible.

"Fortunately it is not allowed to colour couverture in Switzerland." – "What do you mean?" –
"Well, otherwise Franz might have painted us lilac after all."

# GORILLA

Body:      Couverture, cut out
Base:      Couverture, cut out
Head       Couverture shell, Ø = 5 cm / 1.97 in.
Ears:      Couverture half-shell, Ø = 2.1 cm / 0.82 in.
Mouth:     Couverture egg, 4.4 x 2.7 cm / 1.73 x 1.06 in.
Nose:      Modelling couverture
Hair:      Modelling couverture
Hand:      Modelling couverture
Banana:    Marzipan
Weight:    80 g / 2.8 oz.

The body can either be cut out with a knife or a form made of band-iron. The slightly open mouth gives the gorilla a funny and more lively look.

Due to the low weight, the gorilla is good value for money and a certain top seller.

"For our role in 'Gorillas in the mist' we were given so many bananas as salary that we nearly fell sick."

# MASK

Face:    Couverture, moulded mask
Scarf:    Modelling couverture,
            1.5 mm / 0.05 in. thick, 13 cm / 5.1 in. wide,
            length depending on the mould

The moderately prized mould for the face can be bought in hobby shops.

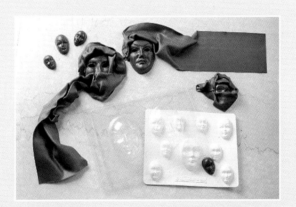

Warm the modelling couverture for the scarf in the microwave oven for a few seconds and knead well. Roll out to 1.5 mm / 0.05 in. on the rolling machine, cut in strips and wrap around the mask as long as the modelling couverture is still flexible.

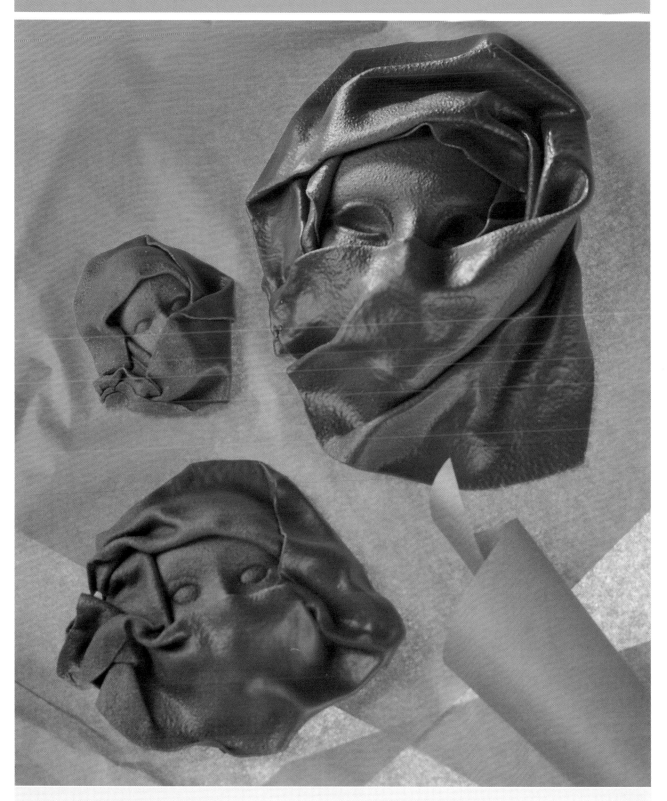

"Leather masks offered by a market trader were the inspiration for these masks."

The relief mould for the face can be bought in hobby shops. Normally it is cast with plaster or porcelain.

Face: Couverture, moulded mask
Back of
the head: Half egg of couverture, size corresponding to the face mask
Shoulders: Couverture half-shell
Hat: Couverture, moulded cylinder
Hair: Rice crispies
Dress: White decoration mass, rolled to 1 mm / 0.0394 in.

An egg form happened to fit perfectly to these faces as back of the head. Only at the neck the egg had to be slightly melted to form.

The light rice Crispies are used for the hair. Tempered couverture and some liquid cocoa butter are mixed with the Rice Crispies and immediately portioned with a spoon. The hair is fastened to the head before spraying.

"What has come over Ziegler to stick rice crispies to my ears?"

| Body: | Couverture egg, |
| --- | --- |
| | 3.8 x 6.2 cm / 1.49 x 2.44 in. |
| Head: | Couverture shell, Ø = 5 cm / 1.97 in. |
| Feet: | Couverture egg, 3.3 x 2 cm / 1.29 x 0.78 in. |
| Ears: | Modelling couverture |
| Wings: | Couverture, stencilled |
| Muzzle: | Half-shells, Ø = 2 cm / 0.78 in. |
| Hair: | Modelling couverture, pressed through |
| | a garlic press |
| Teeth: | White modelling mass |
| Nose: | Rose marzipan |
| Base: | Couverture, moulded baking tin |
| Weight: | 75 g / 2.64 oz. |

Bats normally belong to the less attractive animals. These two specimens are just the opposite: all ready to bite into. By stencilling the wings, one of the most time-consuming jobs can be shortened and the figure can be produced in an efficient way.

"Whose idea was it to hang me up headfirst into the photo?"
"But it looks good." "Maybe, but I've got problems while eating."
"What problems?" "I can hardly swallow."

| Body: | Couverture egg, |
|---|---|
| | 8.3 x 5.4 cm / 3.26 x 2.12 in. |
| Head: | Couverture half-shell, Ø = 6 cm / 2.36 in. |
| Trunk: | Marzipan, pressed into a silicone form, |
| | 25 g / 0.88 in. |
| Ears: | Couverture, stencilled |
| Hair: | Modelling couverture, pressed through |
| | a garlic press |
| Tusks: | White modelling couverture |
| Base: | Couverture, Ø = 6 cm / 2.36 in. |
| Weight: | 130 g / 4.58 oz. |

These elephants have a compact form and the saleswoman will certainly take pleasure in packing it.

By spraying, the marzipan trunk receives the same colour as the rest of the body; moreover the marzipan is thus sealed and remains soft for a long time.

"Why do these safari tourists stare at us like that?
Come on, let's ram the jeep and thoroughly shake them about."

| Body: | Couverture, moulded champagne glass |
|---|---|
| Head: | Couverture shell, Ø = 6 cm / 2.36 in. |
| Shoes: | Couverture egg, 4.3 x 2.7 cm / 1.69 x 1.06 in. |
| Hands: | Couverture egg, 4.3 x 2.7 cm / 1.69 x 1.06 in. |
| Thumb: | Couverture egg, 3.1 x 2.2 cm / 0.86 in. |
| Satchel: | Modelling couverture |
| Glasses: | Hollow body for chocolates, stuck together by melting |
| Baseball cap: | Modelling couverture, Ø = 6.5 cm / 2.55 in. and 4.5 cm / 1.77 in. |
| Letters: | Couverture |

The plastic moulds for the letters are from the toy shop.

The structure of a figure made of pipes or a cylinder and a shell is not new. The plastic champagne glasses used as moulds, however, allow to quickly produce these figures.

Baseball caps give all figures a juvenile and funny expression. And a satchel completes the figure.

"Mum, did you remember my peanut butter-jelly sandwich?"

# CHRISTMAS TREE

Tree body:     Couverture, moulded cone
Trunk:         Hollow body for chocolates,
               21 mm / 0.82 in. high
Gift parcel:   Marzipan
Top of tree:   Truffle shell
Nose:          Truffle shell
Weight:        92 g / 3.24 oz

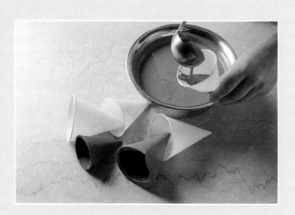

My continuous search for ideal and simple moulds was crowned with success with regards to this cone. Cones of this kind made of paper and sealed with wax serve as drinking cups in the USA.

A base is fixed to the cone and the 21 mm / 0.82 in. high hollow form for chocolates serves as trunk. The figure is sprayed with untempered couverture and immediately sprinkled with grated couverture. This gives the cone a rougher structure. The X-mas tree is then frozen onto it and sprayed again.

"The gifts for the children become heavier every year.
What about a pay rise?"

# SNAIL

Body:     Couverture pipe, Ø = 2.3 cm / 0.9 in.
Head:     Couverture shell, Ø = 4.2 cm / 1.65 in.
Nose:     Couverture egg, 4.5 x 2.6 cm / 1.77 x 1.02 in.
Mouth:    Modelling couverture
          2 mm / 0.08 in. thick, Ø = 3 cm / 1.18 in.
Eyes:     Mini truffle shell, Ø = 2 cm / 0.78 in.
Feelers:  Modelling couverture, 6 g / 0.21 oz. each
Shell:    Couverture shell, Ø = 7.7 cm / 3.03 in.,
          strongly melted,
          couverture half-shell, Ø = 4.2 cm / 1.65 in.
          couverture half-shell, Ø = 2.3 cm / 0.9 in.
Weight:   175 g / 6.17 oz.

This snail is one of the favourite figures of the author. The figure owes its attractivity to the shell, the nose and especially the intensive expression of the ball-shaped eyes.

To avoid that the shell becomes too weighty, the large shell is strongly melted. This results in a slimmer form.

72

The figures by the comic artist Mordillo inspired the author to create this figure, especially the ball-shaped eyes.

# BIRD WITH HAT

| | |
|---|---|
| Body: | Couverture egg, 8.2 x 5.4 cm |
| Head: | Couverture half-shell, Ø = 6 cm / 2.36 in. |
| Tail feather: | Couverture wedge, cut out |
| Hat: | Disk, Ø = 8 cm / 3.14 in. |
| | pre-fabricated speciality bowl |
| | Ø = 5 cm / 1.97 in. |
| Wings: | Piped with thickened couverture |
| Front |
| feathers: | Couverture drops, combed |
| Beak: | Marzipan |
| Feet: | Marzipan |
| Weight: | 155 g / 5.47 oz. |

Sketch the desired form of the wings on a piece of paper prior to piping them and put it under a sheet of silicone paper. Patterns are ideal and allow to work very precisely. To prevent the thickened couverture from running together, pipe the outer feather first and then the middle one. Wait a minute before you pipe the two remaining feathers.

For the front feathers pipe a drop of thickened couverture onto the paper and draw the desired structure with a comb. If you want curly hair, put the combed couverture into a half-round baking tin immediately.

"I have already been practising. Soon I will have my first flying lesson.
A crash helmet would perhaps be more appropriate than Daddy's best hat."

# JUMPING BUNNY

| | |
|---|---|
| Body: | Couverture egg, 8.2 x 5.5 cm / 3.22 x 2.16 in. |
| Head: | Couverture shell, Ø = 6 cm / 2.36 in. |
| Foreleg: | Couverture egg, 6.2 x 3.8 cm / 2.44 x 1.5 in. |
| Hind leg: | Couverture egg, 4.4 x 2.6 cm / 1.73 x 1.02 in. |
| Ears: | Couverture egg, 6.2 x 3.8 cm / 2.44 x 1.5 in. |
| Tail: | Couverture egg, 3.3 x 2 cm / 1.29 x 0.78 in. |
| Muzzle: | Couverture egg, 4.5 x 2.6 cm / 1.77 x 1.02 in. |
| Hair: | Marzipan |
| Weight: | 145 g / 5.11 oz. |

The cheeks and the tail are made of white couverture; this gives the bunny an interesting colour nuance and livens up the figure. The pad should not be hollow and is therefore solidly cast and decorated.

The veining of the beam is made with the socalled "Maser Boy". Originally used as a painter's tool, the "Maser Boy" more and more makes its entry in confectionery business. Pour some couverture on a smooth surface and make the veining by jiging movements.

"I just had my hair bleached.
Well, I didn't want to look like all other rabbits running around."

# NOSEY BUNNY

| | |
|---|---|
| Body: | Couverture egg, 8.2 x 5.5 cm / 3.22 x 2.16 in. |
| Cheeks: | Couverture egg, 4.3 x 2.5 cm / 0.98 in. |
| Head: | Couverture egg, 8.2 x 5.5 cm / 3.22 x 2.16 in. |
| Ears: | Couverture, piped |
| Arms: | Couverture, piped |
| Feet: | Couverture, piped |
| Nose: | Couverture egg, 3.3 x 2 cm / 1.29 x 0.78 in. |
| Weight: | 145 g / 5.11 oz. |

The rabbit is produced in an efficient way.
The ears, forelegs and hind legs are piped.
The pointed form of the head gives the rabbit a curious and nosey look.

Body:       Couverture, moulded one-way white wine glass
Head:       Couverture shell, Ø = 6 cm / 2.36 in.
Cheeks:     Couverture egg, 4.5 x 2.6 cm / 1.77 x 1.02 in.
            Couverture half-shell, Ø = 2.3 cm / 0.9 in.
Ears:       Boat-shaped cover foil, peeled off
Teeth:      White modelling mass
Weight:     95 g / 3.35 oz.

One more possible mould: the white wine glass. The body thus moulded is melted at an angle, which gives these rabbits their shy but curious look.

The manufacturing process of the ears by means of a cover stencil for prefabricated boat-shaped pastry shells is uniquely efficient and fascinating. Stencil the ears on strips of silicone paper and immediately put into a half-round form for cut pralines.

"You know, I almost die of shame for my projecting teeth." –
"Let's go to the dentist tomorrow, perhaps he will fit us with a brace."

# LION

Body: Canache, piped
Plate: Couverture plate, 7 x 11 cm / 2.75 x 4.33 in.
Head: Couverture half-shell, Ø = 4.2 cm / 1.65 in.
Cheeks: Couverture half-shell, Ø = 2 cm / 0.78 in.
Feet: Truffle shells, melted
Tail: Marzipan, 5 g / 0.17 oz.
Mane: Marzipan, 2 mm / 0.08 in. thick,
cut out and stuck on
Base: Couverture plate (same form as mane)
Weight: 110 g / 3.88 oz.

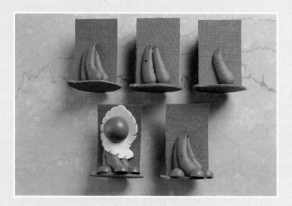

Pipe soft-stirred canache with an 11-mm nozzle on the prepared couverture plates. If you pipe the body with some sweep, the figure will gain a more elegant and lively appearance. After spraying, the white marzipan slightly shimmers through and gives the mane a beautiful light shading.

Sketching and cutting out of stencils is not very time-consuming and guarantees regular results.

"Originally we wanted to recite for the movie 'The Lion King'.
But they warned us that the hyenas are absolutely mad about chocolate.
So we took the by far less glamorous job in 'Magic Chocolate'."

| | |
|---|---|
| Fuselage: | Couverture, moulded champagne glass |
| | Couverture half-shell, Ø = 5 cm / 1.97 in. |
| Lower wings: | Couverture, cut out, (14 x 2.5 cm / 0.98 in.) |
| Wheels: | Couverture shell, Ø = 2.5 cm / 0.98 in. |
| Propeller: | Couverture, cut out |
| Top wings: | Couverture, cut out |
| Nose: | Couverture half-shell, Ø = 2.5 cm / 0.98 in. |
| Flying glasses: | Modelling couverture |
| Weight: | 110 g / 3.88 oz. |

Melt the moulded champagne glass form so that the half-shell fits seamless to the fuselage.

Cut through the lower wings twice so they fit exactly to the fuselage.

"Charles Lindbergh would have been delighted at the sight of us.
But I doubt whether he would have dared to cross the Atlantic Ocean with us."

# CAMEL

Body: 2 couverture eggs,
6.2 x 3.8 cm / 2.44 x 1.5 in.
Head: Couverture shell, Ø = 4.2 cm / 1.65 in.
Muzzle: Couverture egg, 6.2 x 3.8 cm / 2.44 x 1.49 in.
Couverture egg, 4.5 x 2.6 cm / 1.77 x 1.02 in.
Feet: Couverture shell, Ø = 2.5 cm / 0.98 in.
Ears: Marzipan
Hair: Marzipan, pressed through a garlic press
Blanket: Marzipan
Pyramides: Couverture
Weight: 100 g / 3.53 oz

The typical humps are made by melting two eggs and sticking them together; and the blanket in earthy colours reminds the viewer of caravans and the sandy deserts of North Africa.

The hump on the muzzle together with the humps on the back give this figure the other, typical camel characteristic.

"Are you fit for the big camel race on the weekend?" –
"Yes, I feel great! Last week I did the altitude training in Timbuktu."

# DON MARTIN

Head:        Couverture, moulded plastic bottle
Shoulders:   Couverture half-shell, Ø = 6 cm / 2.36 in.
Eyes:        Couverture egg,
             3.1 x 2.1 cm / 1.22 x 0.82 in.
Eye lids:    Modelling couverture, Ø = 3 cm / 1.18 in.
Ears:        Modelling couverture, 3 g / 0.1 oz. each
Nose:        Modelling couverture, 5 g / 0.17 oz.
Hat:         Couverture half-shell, Ø = 6 cm / 2.36 in.
Brim
of hat:      Modelling couverture, Ø = 8 cm / 3.14 in.

Even a plastic bottle can be used as casting mould. Here the slim high form is the basic element for the head of the comic figure. This form can also be used as body for a slim figure.

Don Martin from the Comic 'MAD' and this figure are as like as two peas. The eye brows, which are very important for the funny character of the head and the mouth, are cut out with a warm knife. The eye lids are fixed after spraying.

"Just now it was possible to drink out of my head,
and now I am cast in chocolate. Absolutely nothing is sacred to Ziegler!"

Chocolate
box:       Couverture, Ø = 12 cm / 4,72 in.
Lid:       Couverture, Ø = 14 cm / 5.51 in.
Half moon: Couverture, moulded deep-drawn form
Contents:  Cut pralines
Weight:    300 g / 10.59 oz. (incl. contents)

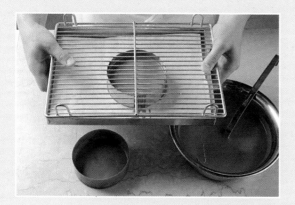

Do you want to precisely and quickly manufacture a chocolate box? Put a cake ring on a
baking tin, fill in couverture, cover with a wire
rack and turn over. Repeat this procedure
twice. The smoother the material and the
seam of the cake ring, the easier can the
couverture be demoulded.

Spread couverture on the star foil now available on the market for the lid decoration. Cut
out disks as soon as the couverture is getting
hard. Let harden in the refrigerator. The silk
screen printing design comes off the foil and
produces a fascinating decoration.

"Take note of how the background colour gives this product an exclusive image."

# TURTLE

Shell:     Couverture egg,
             7.4 x 5.7 cm / 2.91 x 2.24 in.
Head:     Couverture half-shell, Ø = 6 cm / 2.36 in.
             Couverture half-shell, Ø = 5 cm / 1.97 in.
Nose:     Couverture egg,
             4.5 x 2.6 cm / 1.77 x 1.02 in.
Eyes:     Truffle shell, Ø = 2.5 cm / 0.98 in.
Tail fins:  Modelling couverture, 16 g / 0.56 oz. each
Front fins: Modelling couverture, 35 g / 1.23 oz. each
Neck:     Modelling couverture, 30 g / 1.05 oz.
Hat:      Marzipan, 20 g / 0.7 oz.

For the shell slightly spray a structured egg form with milk couverture. Then fill in white couverture.

For the head two different shell sizes are used. Thus the lower jaw is displaced to the back.

"How old were you yesterday?" – "112!" "Well, so you are in the prime of life."

# BELL BOY

| | |
|---|---|
| Body: | Couverture, moulded champagne glass |
| Head: | Couverture shell, Ø = 6 cm / 2.36 in. |
| Feet: | Couverture egg, 6.2 x 3.8 cm / 2.44 x 1.49 in. / 2.44 x 1.5 in. |
| Neck: | Couverture pipe |
| Hair: | Vermicelle flakes |
| Hat: | Speciality bowl |
| Hands: | Modelling couverture, 20 g / 0.7 oz. |
| Ears: | Modelling couverture |
| Coat: | Modelling couverture |
| Suitcase: | Marzipan |

The author dedicates this figure to all bell boys, who have to carry his heavy suitcases.

The suitcases are cut out from a marzipan block. Half of the head is brushed with couverture and dipped into chocolate flakes.

The champagne glass form for the body is placed with the opening pointing upwards. Thus the page looks a little stronger.

"If only Ziegler could keep to the weight limit for suitcases.
He pays no heed to my intervertebral disk and over and above I am not given a tip."

Body:      Couverture egg, 6.2 x 3.8 cm / 2.44 x 1.5 in.
Head:      Couverture shell, Ø = 5 cm / 1.97 in.
Front paw: Couverture egg, 3.3 x 2 cm / 1.29 x 0.78 in.
Hind paw:  Couverture egg, 4.5 x 2.6 cm / 1.77 x 1.02 in.
Tail:      Marzipan, 12 g / 0.42 oz.
Ears:      Couverture egg, 3.3 x 2 cm / 1.29 x 0.78 in.
Hair:      Marzipan
Basket:    Couverture

Pipe thickened couverture into aluminium moulds, clean the brim with a scraper and let harden.

The chiselled muzzle and the hair are modelled with marzipan, separately sprayed and are fixed at the end. The hair can either be pressed through a garlic press or rolled by hand. The second method makes them look a bit more weighty.

"Garfield stood me up again.
McDonald's round the corner probably again had a magic attraction on him."

Chocolate

| | |
|---|---|
| Box: | Couverture |
| Lid: | Couverture, spread on printed foil |
| Ball: | Couverture |
| Decorations: | Couverture |

To get a ball that looks like a planet, brush some milk couverture into a half-shell mould. The brushstrokes must still be visible. Fill ball with white couverture.

This box with modern design is suited for all occasions.
With some alterations it can also be used for seasonal activities.

# INDIVIDUAL PIECES

As soon as you have aquired reknown as a designer for creative chocolate figures, it won't take long and societies, companies or private persons will ask for special orders.

Now you have the chance to become known even beyond the town boundary.

If possible, you should try to accept all special orders. In most of the cases these works are presented and admired in a circle of persons. The mouth-to-mouth propaganda is generally acknowledged to be the best advertising.

Therefore it must be recommended to keep some of the most frequently used egg shells, balls, cylinders, etc. in cast form in stock, so that you can begin to "assemble" the figure at once, because it is undisputed that most of the time is lost by the provision of the required material.

Take care to keep the production simple so that the price for the "work of art" remains payable, although the customers are normally quite aware of the fact that special orders have their price.

# PENGUIN

| | |
|---|---|
| Head: | Couverture shell, Ø = 9.5 cm / 3.74 in. |
| Body: | Couverture egg, 16 x 10 cm / 6.29 x 3.93 in. |
| Arms: | Couverture, cut out and bend |
| Mouth: | Modelling couverture, Ø = 6.5 cm / 2.55 in. |
| Feet: | Modelling couverture, 25 g / 0.88 oz. each |
| Eye brows: | Modelling couverture, 25 g / 0.88 oz. each |
| Cloth: | White decoration modelling mass |
| Belly: | White decoration modelling mass |
| Coupe glass: | Couverture, moulded champagne glass |

The yellow eye brows that are typical for the "Rockhopper" penguin are made of coloured modelling couverture, which allows to cut out detailled ornaments; moreover the brows become more stable. The same applies to the mouth. If you use marzipan for a mouth of this size, you would have to allow the marzipan to dry a little before it can be fastened.

The wings are cut out. To prevent the wings from breaking, they have to be put over a naked flame for a split second. This technique requires some experience – but the worst that can happen is that the couverture becomes too soft.

"Well guys, who ordered an Eskimo flip?"

| Body: | Couverture egg, 6.2 x 3.8 cm / 2.44 x 1.49 in. |
|---|---|
| Head: | Couverture shell, Ø = 5 cm / 1.97 in. |
| Legs: | Couverture pipes, length of each section 4.5 cm / 1.77 in. |
| Feet: | Couverture egg, 3.1 x 2.1 cm / 1.22 x 0.82 in. |
| Weight: | 105 g/3.7 oz. |

Cut solid cast couverture pipes into 16 evenly long pieces. At the joins the pieces must be melted at an angle and stuck together. Fitting the legs in a more regular or more irregular way will change the posture of the spider: it is more or less in motion.

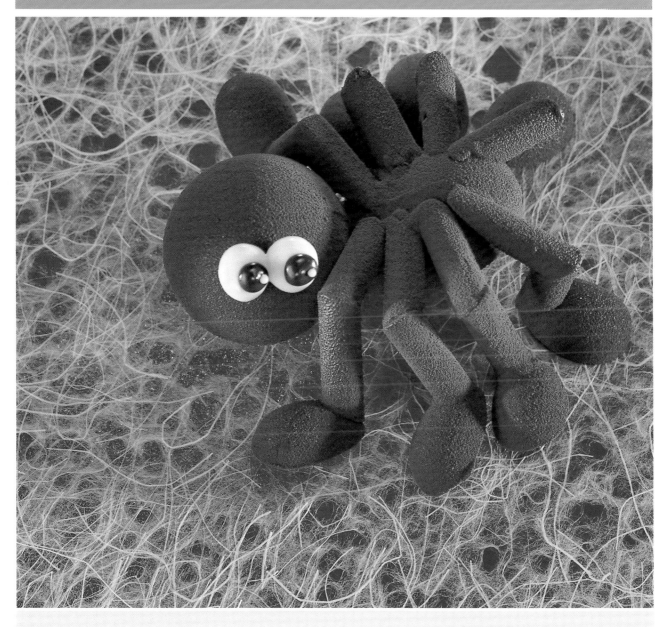

"O.K., o.K., o.K., no panic, I won't creep out of the photo.
Besides, if you don't like the sight of me, just turn over the page."

Body:       Couverture, moulded champagne glass
Head:       Couverture egg,
            4.5 x 2.6 cm / 1.77 x 1.02 in.
Muzzle:     Couverture egg, 6.2 x 3.8 cm / 2.44 x 1.5 in.
Fore legs:  Couverture pipes
Thighs:     Couverture egg, 6.2 x 3.8 cm / 2.44 x 1.5 in.
Hind legs:  Couverture egg,
            4.5 x 2.6 cm / 1.77 x 1.02 in.
Forelegs:   Couverture egg, 3.3 x 2 cm / 1.29 x 0.78 in.
Ears:       Modelling couverture
Muzzle:     Wrapped in modelling couverture
Head:       Wrapped in modelling couverture
Body:       Wrapped in modelling couverture
Weight:     190 g / 6.7 oz.

The champagne glass here serves as a body for the dog. The muzzle should be very characteristic; for that reason the size must be accordingly large.

Modelling couverture is used for details that influence the dog's special look. After that the dog is sprayed with untempered couverture and sprinkled with grated couverture. The general impression is perfected by spraying the frozen figure.

"In the dog show I was only placed second.
It's incredible that the jury considered the pinscher to be more attractive than me!"

# MUSICIAN

Musician:   Couverture, solid casting
Record:     Couverture, solid casting
Notes:      Couverture shell, Ø = 5 cm / 1.97 in.
            Couverture pipes

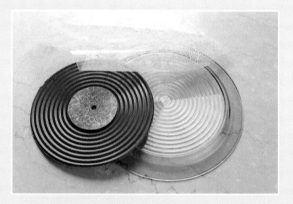

This singer is solidly cast. For that reason the crystallization in the refrigerator lasts much longer than with any other form, because the silicone of this form has a strong isolating effect in contrary to other materials.

Due to the details of the hand, a cut has to be made into the silicone, since otherwise the microphone and the hand could not be uncovered. Uneven spots at the edges are cleaned with a knife.

Long live the plastic age! Numerous cheap articles of daily use can be used as casting moulds for our purposes – which can only be recognized on close inspection. The form and the grooves of a vinyl record had been created with this base of a plate.

Who said that heavy metal musicians haven't got much upstairs?
This rocker is full of finest couverture, filled right to the top.

# FROG

| | |
|---|---|
| Body: | Couverture egg, 8.3 x 5.4 cm / 3.26 x 2.12 in. |
| Head: | Couverture shell, Ø = 6 cm / 2.36 in. |
| Thighs: | Couverture egg, 4.3 x 2.7 cm / 1.69 x 1.06 in. |
| Eyes: | Truffle shells |
| Glasses: | Hollow shells for pralines, melted |
| Hands: | Modelling couverture, 8 g / 0.28 oz. each |
| Feet: | Modelling couverture, 10 g / 0.35 oz. each |

When brushing a leaf, always take the rear side, because here are the stronger ribs. Brush three or four times. Detailed originals like this leaf are normally destructed when you peel off the couverture. More simple leaves can be used several times.

The open muzzle is made by strongly melting one side of the two half-shells. The sun glasses have a surprisingly simple structure, but a

great effect. Hollow shells for pralines are strongly melted and stuck together with a drop of couverture.

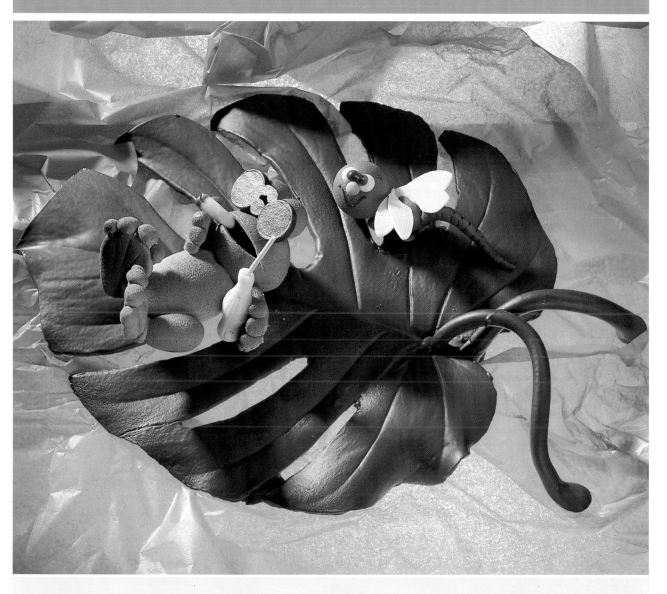

"My brother Kermit may be more famous than me and Miss Piggy may be his girl-friend.
But I have got no stress and I deny myself nothing."

**Kangaroo:**

| | |
|---|---|
| Body: | Couverture, moulded piping bag holder |
| Head: | Couverture egg, 11 x 7.4 cm / 4.33 x 2.91 in. |
| Mouth: | Couverture egg, 8.3 x 5.4 cm / 3.26 x 2.12 in. |
| Thighs: | Couverture egg, 6.7 x 10 cm |
| Pouch: | Modelling couverture |
| Arms: | Couverture egg, 6.2 x 3.8 cm / 2.44 x 1.5 in. |
| Feet: | Couverture egg, 8.3 x 5.4 cm / 3.26 x 2.12 in. |
| Hands: | Couverture egg, 6.2 x 3.8 cm / 2.44 x 1.5 in. |
| Ears: | Couverture egg, 6.2 x 3.8 cm / 2.44 x 1.5 in. |
| Lip: | Modelling couverture, Ø = 4.5 cm / 1.77 in. |

**Kangaroo Baby**

| | |
|---|---|
| Body: | Couverture egg, 6.2 x 3.8 cm / 2.44 x 1.5 in. |
| Mouth: | Couverture egg, 4.5 x 2.6 cm / 1.77 x 1.02 in. |
| Hands: | Couverture egg, 4.5 x 2.6 cm / 1.77 x 1.02 in. |
| Ears: | Couverture egg, 3.3 x 2 cm / 1.29 x 0.78 in. |

**Koala**

| | |
|---|---|
| Body: | Couverture egg, 12 x 7.8 cm / 4.72 x 3.07 in. |
| Head: | Couverture shell, Ø = 4.7 cm / 1.85 in. |
| Thighs: | Couverture egg, 6.2 x 3.8 cm / 2.44 x 1.5 in. |
| Arms: | Couverture egg, 4.5 x 2.6 cm / 1.77 x 1.02 in. |
| Nose: | Couverture egg, 4.5 x 2.6 cm / 1.77 x 1.02 in. |
| Ears: | Modelling couverture, Ø = 4.7 cm / 1.85 in. |
| Feet: | Modelling couverture, 25 g / 0.88 oz. each |
| Hands: | Modelling couverture, 25 g / 0.88 oz. each |
| Mouth: | Modelling couverture, Ø = 3 cm / 1.18 in. |
| Eye brows: | Modelling couverture, Ø = 3 cm / 1.18 in. |

**Kangaroo**

The form of the piping bag holder gives the animal a somewhat stiff posture. To liven up the figure, special attention was paid to the production of the kangaroo baby. This is where the second look is cast. Spraying the frozen figure results in the typical rust-brown colour of the kangaroo.

**Koala**

The typical oval nose of the koala is fixed after spraying. The shading on the belly was made with an airbrush.

Koala: "Why have you been called kangaroo?"
Kangoroo: "Well, the British explorers asked the Aborigines, what they call the jumping animals.
The Aborigines answered with kangaroo, which means as much as: 'I can't understand you'.
The clever explorers then told the whole world that we are called kangaroos."

# HEN

Body: Couverture egg, 8.3 x 5.4 cm / 3.26 x 2.12 in.
Head: Couverture egg, 6.2 x 3.8 cm / 2.44 x 1.5 in.
Neck: Couverture pipe
Wing: Modelling couverture
Legs: Modelling couverture
Claws: Modelling couverture
Neck ring: Modelling couverture
Comb: Marzipan, 3 g / 0.1 oz. each
Beak: Marzipan, 5 g / 0.17 oz.
Weight: 170 g / 6 oz.

The retroposition of the body gives this hen a listless impression. Working out such details makes the success of a figure.

The fiery Spanish cockerel by Antonio Escriba was copied, to have this picture tell a story. The figure is nearly 30 years old, but in the author's opinion, it still is the best cockerel that has ever been created.

# SEAL

Body:      Couverture egg, 10 x 6.7 cm / 3.93 x 2.36 in.
Head:      Couverture shell, Ø = 6 cm / 2.36 in.
Front fins: Couverture egg, 4.5 x 2.6 cm / 1.77 x 1.02 in.
Tail fins:  Couverture egg, 4.5 x 2.6 cm / 1.77 x 1.02 in.
Muzzle:    Couverture shell, Ø = 2.5 cm / 0.98 in.
Nose:      Modelling couverture

**Baby Seal**
Body:    Couverture egg, 6.2 x 3.8 cm / 2.44 x 1.5 in.
Head:    Couverture shell, Ø = 4.2 cm / 1.65 in.
Fins:    Modelling couverture
Muzzle:  Couverture shell, Ø = 2 cm / 0.78 in.
         strongly melted

Cut a white couverture block with a knife to the form of an ice floe. The body of the baby seal is fastened directly to the ice floe.

The tail and front fins of the baby seal are made of modelling couverture in the form of a drop. Marzipan is not suited for this purpose, because it does not have the same colour as the white couverture and cannot be covered by spraying.

To fix the head firmly to the body of the seal, warm a ladle (Ø = 6 cm / 2.36 in.) over a flame and melt a hole into the body. The head is put into the opening. Depending on the way you fix the couverture shell, the posture of the body or the head can be altered.

"And now, my little one, firmly clap your fins and you will get a herring."

Body:          Marzipan, 55 g / 1.94 oz.
Belly:         Marzipan, 10 g / 0.35 oz.
Head:          Marzipan, 30 g / 1.05 oz.
Muzzle:        Marzipan, 2 g / 0.07 oz.
Arms:          Marzipan, 12 g / 0.42 oz.
Legs:          Marzipan, 12 g / 0.42 oz.
Nose:          Marzipan, 4 g / 0.14 oz.
Ear:           Marzipan, 4 g / 0.14 oz.
Hat:           Marzipan, 18 g / 0.63 oz.
Brim of hat: Marzipan, 18 g / 0.63 oz.
Planet:        Couverture half-shell, Ø = 13.5 cm / 5.31 in.
Moon:          Couverture crescent, Ø = 14 cm / 5.5 in.

Melt out holes of different diameters from the half-shell using pastry cutters. Close these holes with half-shells of the same size, which are fixed from behind.

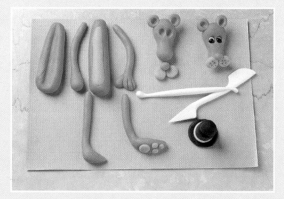

The sticks shown above are most commonly used modelling devices. Use writing chocolate for the eyes of the panther. Ordinary couverture would not generate such beautifully protruding pupils.

"Since Peter Sellers departed this life, there is not so much talk about me anymore. Now I am in a waiting position and hope that a producer wants to make another film with me."

# DOG

Body:      Couverture egg, 12 x 7.8 cm / 4.72 x 3.07 in.
Head:      Couverture shell, Ø = 7.6 cm / 2.99 in.
Muzzle:    Couverture, moulded mask
Ears:      Couverture, cut out
Thighs:    Couverture egg, 6.2 x 3.7 cm / 2.44 x 1.45 in.
Hind paw:  Couverture egg, 6.2 x 3.7 cm / 2.44 x 1.45 in.
Bone:      Couverture, consisting of a pipe, two shells (Ø = 5 cm / 1.97 in.)
           and two egg moulds (8.3 x 5.4 cm / 3.26 x 2.12 in.)

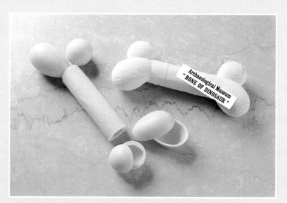

The muzzle of the dog is based on a carnival mask of rubber. During carnival these masks can be found in all toy shops. This form must be fully cast, because if you only cast a thin-walled layer, the couverture would break when peeling off the mask.

Bone: Put together all parts and brush. This will level out all uneven spots and the brush-strokes give the bone an additional structure.

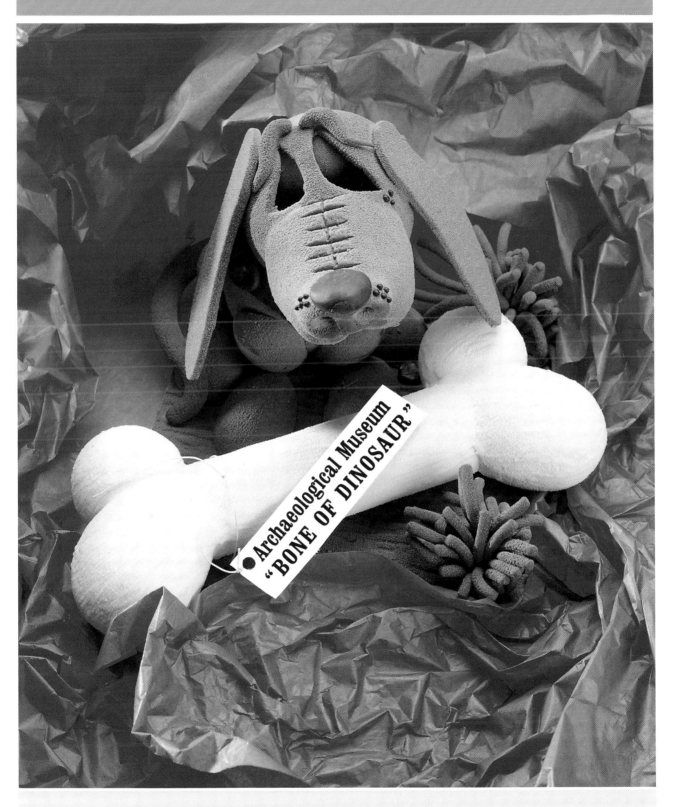

"Mr. Spielberg, don't look at me so angry. 'Jurassic Park' is just finished and I thought that I could perhaps keep a little requisite."

# DINOSAUR

Body: Couverture egg, 10 x 6.7 cm / 3.93 x 2.36 in.
Head: Couverture egg, 8.3 x 5.4 cm / 3.26 x 2.12 in.
Muzzle: Couverture egg, 8.3 x 5.4 cm / 3.26 x 2.12 in.
Cheek: Couverture egg, 3.3 x 2 cm / 1.29 x 0.78 in.
Thighs: Couverture egg, 6.2 x 3.8 cm / 2.44 x 1.5 in.
Tail: Modelling couverture, 1.5 mm / 0.05 in. thick
Back comb: Couverture, cut out with praline cutter
Dino spots: Green marzipan,
cut out through plastic foil
Weight: 300 g / 10.59 oz.

Instead of forming the tail of modelling couverture, you could also use a cast champagne glass form. Modelling couverture, however, allows to give the tail of the dinosaur a more lively look, because the end of the tail can still be bent.

The thighs are fixed at the joins between tail and body. The individual parts of the back comb are cut out with a praline cutter and staggered.

"Get out of your egg, the rehearsal for 'Jurassic Park 2' will begin in half an hour."

# TOUCAN

Body:      Couverture egg, 10 x 6.7 cm / 3.93 x 2.36 in.
Head:      Couverture half-shell, Ø = 6 cm / 2.36 in.
Beak:      Couverture, moulded mask
Wings:     Modelling couverture
Eyes:      Truffle shells, Ø = 2.5 cm / 0.98 in.
Trunk:     Couverture pipe

The form for the beak of the toucan is a carnival mask, which was found in a toy shop.
Solidly cast the mask since otherwise the
plastic cannot be removed.

Thickly cover the pipe for the trunk with
couverture and mark the structure of the rind
immediately afterwards.

"The photographer just told me to keep still and hold my tongue.
Now he can wait for my friendly smile as long as he likes.
He can say 'Smile' as often as he wants."

| Bathtub: | Couverture half-shell, Ø = 13.5 cm / 5.31 in. |
| Bathtub feet: | Modelling couverture |
| Head: | Couverture shell, Ø = 5 cm / 1.97 in. |
| Ears: | Modelling couverture |
| Nose: | Small truffle shell, Ø = 2 cm / 0.78 in. |
| Foam bath: | Rice crispies, mixed with white couverture |
| Hair: | Modelling couverture, pressed through a garlic press |
| Flippers: | Rose modelling couverture |
| Hands: | Modelling couverture |
| Sun glasses: | Praline cover stencil, peeled off |
| Diver's goggles: | Oval hollow shells for pralines, strongly melted |
| Snorkel: | Modelling couverture |

Whenever you are longing for a warm holiday resort, it must be foggy and cold outside. The foam bath is made of rice crispies, white couverture and some cocoa butter.

The couverture for the bathroom floor is spread on plexiglass (from the hardware shop), which is normally used as light covering. Thinly spread white couverture, let harden and spread a second layer of dark couverture.

"Mary, listen, a bungalow directly on the beach, all inclusive for less than 1000 dollars,—.
It's crazy! Hurry up and pack the suitcases."

# GEISHA

| Body: | Couverture egg, 8.3 x 5.4 cm / 3.26 x 2.12 in. |
|-------|------------------------------------------------|
| Legs: | Couverture egg, 4.5 x 2.6 cm / 1.77 x 1.02 in. and 3.3 x 2.1 cm / 1.29 x 0.82 in. |
| Head: | Couverture egg, 6.2 x 3.8 cm / 2.44 x 1.5 in. |
| Dress: | Marzipan |

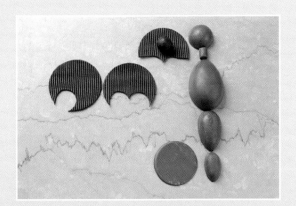

Due to the fragile structure the Geisha was placed among the single pieces. The body could be replaced by a moulded champagne glass. In this case, however, the sweeping element of the figure and the waist would disappear.

The hair is only fastened after spraying. For the kimono light green marzipan is rolled to 2 mm / 0.08 in. The ornaments are cut out from rose marzipan, put onto the green marzipan and rolled again to a thickness of 2 mm / 0.08 in. Thus the two marzipan layers combine well. The white dots are piped later.

"Don't you think that I could be considered to be the
Japanese Kim Basinger with my wasp waist and my pout?"

# SHOWPIECES

The shop window is the best advertising space. You should therefore always take care that the window display attracts the customers. A showpiece being appropriate for the season or any other occasion holds the attention of the viewer and is a perfect eye-catcher. Here you can fully develop your creativity and fantasy.

Whales:     Couverture
Teeth:      White modelling mass
Corals:     Rock sugar

Rock Sugar:
200 g / 7.06 oz.    Water
500 g / 17.65 oz.   Refined sugar
1 tablespoonful     Royal icing

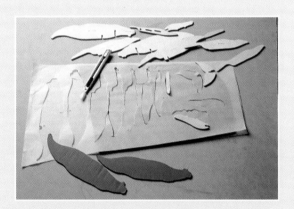

All single elements of the whales are cut out through the paper using a wooden stencil. For this purpose the couverture plate is placed onto a wooden board. Wood is warmer than a marble or chromium-steel table, which gives us more time to cut out the detailed elements.

Boil water and refined sugar in a copper pot to 138 °C / 280 °F. Add the royal icing and quickly stir with a wooden spoon. The volume quickly rises and goes down again. As soon as the mass rises again, fill into a form lined with aluminium foil. Let cool.

Turn rock sugar out of the mould, remove aluminium foil and bring sugar into the desired form by breaking or sawing.

"Hey, little one, get ready for diving!
The Japanese and Norwegian ships tacking up there want to abuse us for scientific experiments."

Firs:      Couverture cone
Sleigh:    Couverture, cut out
Donkey:    Couverture, solid casting

Father Christmas:
Head:      Couverture shell
Body:      Couverture egg
Legs:      Couverture pipes
Arms:      Couverture pipes
Shoes:     Couverture egg
Gloves:    Modelling couverture
Coat:      Modelling couverture
Cap:       Modelling couverture
Beard:     Modelling couverture
Moustache: Modelling couverture

For high cones or thick pipes, spread a layer of couverture on a paper, let harden a little, and than spread the second layer.

Cut the paper with the couverture to form and roll to a cone. To support the form, the cone can be put into a funnel.

Can you imagine Father Christmas without a jute sack? This sack can easily be made. Groove the modelling couverture with a grooving pin and immediately wrap around the egg.

Father Christmas was really stressed, when the young donkey sat down on the sleigh and refused to do his work. What else could he do other than push the sleigh together with the donkey through the woods.
He knew that many shining children's eyes were waiting for him.

| | |
|---|---|
| Rear wall: | Couverture, spread on corrugated sheet |
| Ball: | Couverture, different coloured couvertures applied with brush |
| Lattice: | Modelling couverture |
| Pyramid top: | Couverture, with rusty look |
| Cone: | Couverture |
| Square: | Couverture |
| Semicircles: | Couverture |

**Retiree**

| | |
|---|---|
| Body: | Couverture, cast in a piping bag holder |
| Head: | Couverture egg, 11.3 x 7.6 cm / 4.44 x 2.99 in. |
| Ears: | Couverture egg, 4.5 x 2.6 cm / 1.77 x 1.02 in. |
| Nose: | Truffle shell, Ø = 2.6 cm / 1.02 in. |
| Arms: | Couverture pipes |
| Shoes: | Couverture egg, 11.3 x 7.6 cm / 4.44 x 2.99 in. |
| Hands: | Modelling couverture |
| Coat: | Modelling couverture |
| Dog: | Modelling couverture |

A maximum number of couverture structures are combined in this showpiece. Twelve different ones can be seen in this picture.

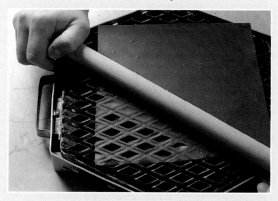

The lattice design of the 'Linzer Torte' is widely known. Roll out modelling couverture and press through the lattice with a rolling pin.

Thinly cover the plastic bubble foil with white couverture. Let it harden in the refrigerator. Lay the couverture on a flat table and carefully remove the plastic. If you want, you can punch out holes with the modelling stick.

Another painter's tool that can be used when working with chocolate: A plastic paint tub (available in every hobby shop).

This 'rusty' looking surface has a very interesting texture. Plastic foil is moistened with water and dusted with cocoa powder. Apply dark couverture and let it harden.

The pensioner found the sculpture rather strange, while his dog already took cover. Is this art or what's it good for?

# UNDERWATER LANDSCAPE

| | |
|---|---|
| Bottom of the sea: | Couverture, spread on a sheet of plastic |
| Base: | Hollow bodies of couverture |
| Sand: | Rice croquant |
| Corals: | Couverture |
| Algae: | Couverture |
| Giant tridacna: | Couverture |

## Black Coral:
A patterned roll that is normally used by a painter, is perfectly suited to create structured surfaces. By rolling several times over the wax paper with a patterned roll that has previously been dipped into couverture you will obtain a structure full of little holes. By piping the coral branches onto this structure, the coral is stabilized and can easily be removed from the wax paper.

## Rock:
Put different hollow bodies of couverture onto a solid couverture plate. Apply couverture on a plastic sheet, spread over the substructure and press against the plate. Let harden and carefully remove the plastic sheet.

**Trumpet Fish:**

Strongly melt the cast funnel so it fits close to a couverture egg. By spraying dark chocolate, the white fish obtains its own colour nuance.

| | |
|---|---|
| Body: | Couverture egg, 8.3 x 5.4 cm / 3.26 x 2.12 in. |
| Trumpet: | Couverture, cast funnel |
| Tail fins: | Couverture, cut out |
| Side fins: | Couverture, cut out |
| Comb: | Couverture, cut out |

**Lobster:**

| | |
|---|---|
| Body: | Couverture egg, 10 x 6.7 cm / 3.93 x 2.36 in. |
| Legs: | Couverture egg, 3.3 x 2 cm / 1.29 x 0.78 in. |
| Tail: | Modelling couverture |
| Nose: | Marzipan |

**Starfish:**

| | |
|---|---|
| Star: | Marzipan |
| Lip: | Marzipan |
| Teeth: | Modelling couverture |

**Puffer:**

| | |
|---|---|
| Body: | Couverture shell, Ø = 6 cm / 2.36 in. |
| Tail fin: | Couverture, cut out |
| Lips: | Modelling couverture |
| Eye brows: | Modelling couverture |
| Side fins: | Couverture, cut out |

**Stingray:**

| | |
|---|---|
| Body: | Couverture egg, 10 x 6.7 cm / 3.93 x 2.36 in. |
| Skin: | Modelling couverture |
| Ray: | Modelling couverture |

**Crab:**

| | |
|---|---|
| Body: | Couverture shell, Ø = 6 cm / 2.36 in. |
| Grip arm: | Modelling couverture |
| Nose: | Modelling couverture |

**Swordfish:**

| | |
|---|---|
| Body: | Couverture egg, 8.3 x 5.4 cm / 3.26 x 2.12 in. |
| Tail fin: | Couverture, cut out |
| Side fin: | Couverture, cut out |
| Sword: | Modelling couverture |

**Horsefish:**

| | |
|---|---|
| Body: | Modelling couverture |
| Back fin: | Modelling couverture |
| Side fin: | Modelling couverture |

**Cuttlefish:**

| | |
|---|---|
| Head: | Couverture egg, 10 x 6.7 cm / 3.93 x 2.36 in. |
| Body: | Couverture shell, Ø = 6 cm / 2.36 in. |
| Tentacles: | Modelling couverture |
| Nose: | Modelling couverture |

**Clam:**

| | |
|---|---|
| Shell: | Modelling couverture |
| Head: | Couverture shell, Ø = 6 cm / 2.36 in. |

**Small Octopus:**

| | |
|---|---|
| Head: | Couverture shell, Ø = 5 cm / 1.97 in. |
| Hat: | Couverture shell, Ø = 6 cm / 2.36 in. |
| Tentacles: | Modelling couverture |

**Sawfish:**

| | |
|---|---|
| Body: | Couverture egg, 8.3 x 5.4 cm / 3.26 x 2.12 in. |
| Back fin: | Couverture, cut out |
| Saw: | Couverture, cut out |
| Side fin: | Couverture, cut out |

**Goggle-Eye:**

| | |
|---|---|
| Body: | Couverture egg, 10 x 6.7 cm / 3.93 x 2.36 in. |
| Mouth: | Modelling couverture |
| Goggle-eyes: | Couverture, cast in a half-shell |
| Fins: | Modelling couverture |

Chessboard: White and dark Gianduja,
rolled to 7 mm / 0.27 in.
squares, 4.5 x 4.5 cm / 1.77 x 1.77 in.

Frame:       Overall dimensions:  50 x 50 cm /
19.68 x 19.68 in.
Inside dimensions:  37 x 37 cm /
14.56 x 14.56 in.

Pawns:       Dice and truffle shells,
3 x 3 x 3 cm / 1.18 x 1.18 x 1.18 in.

Castles:     Dice and pyramides.
3 x 3 x 3 cm / 1.18 x 1.18 x 1.18 in.

Knights:     Dice, 5 x 3 x 3 cm / 1.96 x 1.18 x 1.18 in.,
with bevel cut

Bishops:     Dice and Luna cut praline moulds,
5 x 3 x 3 cm / 1.96 x 1.18 x 1.18 in.

Kings:       Dice and roof-formed cut praline mould
5 x 3 x 3 cm / 1.96 x 1.18 x 1.18 in.

Queens:      Dice and roof-formed cut praline mould
5 x 3 x 3 cm / 1.96 x 1.18 x 1.18 in.

This frame owes its fascinating structure to an embossed wallpaper. Cut the frame to size before you remove the wallpaper. Precise working is the precondition that the black and white squares fit perfectly into the frame.

The clear lines of the chessmen can easily be obtained. Cut a 3 cm / 1.18 in. thick Gianduja plate to dice using a praline guitar; they form the basis for all pieces. Different praline forms, characterizing the individual chessmen, are put onto the dice.

The chess world champion Karpow would probably be a heavyweight,
if he always had to eat all eliminated chessmen.

Nofretete: Couverture, solid casting
Column: Couverture
Cloth: Modelling couverture
1.5 mm / 0.05 in. thick

The column owes its structure to a drain mat for dishes, which can be bought in all department stores.

Since pipes with a large diameter tend to become an oval shape due to their weight, put those pipes into a half-round baking tin and let harden there.

In spring 1995 this showpiece was put on view during a chocolate exhibition in the museum "Swiss Institutes" on the Broadway in New York City.

Frame:          Couverture, solid casting
                Luna cut praline mould
Inner frame:    Couverture plate, cut to a
                rectangle
Tools:          all genuine, but sprayed with
                couvertures

Pralines:       Fine Canache and Gianduja-
                fillings, covered with finest
                Swiss couverture

To offer a praline assortment in a completely different conception, miscellaneously structured bases, which are used for the figures in this book, can also be used for chocolate specialties. Instead of shelving the pralines, they are set off against the background. The cut praline system developed by the author is a very efficient way to give a praline asssortment some new impulses.

The system for the choice of cut pralines is simple, hence the production is very efficient. It opens up completely new possibilities for your fantasy to create your personal and successful "praline design".

The core of the system are plastic moulds with four different profiles (38.5 cm / 15.15 in. long).

**And this is how you do it:**

1. Pipe water-free fillings into the mould using a piping bag.
2. Thoroughly smooth with a pastry knife.
3. Let harden in the refrigerator.
4. Close the bottom with a thin layer of couverture.
5. Remove from the mould, put onto a lattice and cover with couverture after approx. 30 min.
6. Cut to the desired size with a praline guitar before the couverture is completely hard. The length of the mould is adapted to the praline guitar.

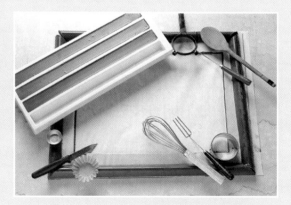

In this case the mould in the illustration is used for the production of a picture frame. Cut a frame out of a couverture plate, put on the cast couverture pipes and stick together by melting. Fix tools from production to the frame and spray several times.

Of all "non-animal" motifs, this is the author's favourite one.

Body:       Couverture egg
Legs:       Couverture pipes
Arms:       Couverture pipes
Shoes:      Couverture egg
Hands:      Couverture egg
Thumbs:     Couverture egg
Head:       Couverture shell
Ears:       Couverture shell
Eye brows:  Modelling couverture
Hat:        Modelling couverture
Apron:      Modelling couverture
Blouse:     Modelling couverture

Thin chocolate walls

Normal chocolate thickness

Thick chocolate walls

Very thick chocolate walls or solidly cast body

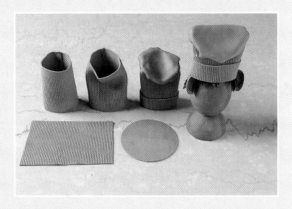

Although the confectioner's hat is not the most important part of this figure, it is a detail that should not be neglected. By buckling the hat in the middle, it gets a dainty look and does not give the impression of being stiff.

The above illustration of the confectioner shows the structure of a bigger figure. The taller the figure, the more stable the basis, that means the legs. The parts are thinner and lighter the higher they are fixed to the figure.

Maybe these two confectioners take the term "making chocolate" in a too literal sense.
This showpiece is the heaviest in weight of the entire book.
The substructure and the rear wall are made of solid couverture.

**Bee:**

Abdomen: Couverture egg, 10 x 6.7cm / 3.93 x 2.36 in.

Upper
body: Couverture egg, 8.3 x 5.4 cm / 3.26 x 2.12 in.

Head: Couverture egg, 10 x 6.7 cm / 3.93 x 2.36 in.

Feet: Couverture half-shell,
Ø = 4.2 cm / 1.65 in. and 5 cm / 1.97 in.
Ø = 4.2 cm / 1.65 in. and 5 cm / 1.97 in.

Cheeks: Couverture egg, 6.2 x 3.8 cm / 2.44 x 1.5 in.

Sting: Modelling couverture

Hands: Modelling couverture, 30 g / 1.05 oz. each

Wings: Couverture

Baseball
cap: Modelling couverture

Flower: Couverture

**Ant:**

Head: Couverture egg, 4.5 x 2.6 cm / 1.77 x 1.02 in.

Legs: Couverture pipe

Feet: Couverture egg, 3.3 x 2 cm / 1.29 x 0.78 in.

Upper
body: Couverture egg, 3.3 x 2 cm / 1.29 x 0.78 in.

Middle
part: Couverture egg, 3.3 x 2 cm / 1.29 x 0.78 in.

Abdomen: Couverture egg, 4.5 x 2.6 cm / 1.77 x 1.02 in.

Feelers: Modelling couverture

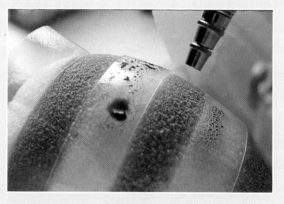

**Ant:**
The little ant, who is watching the bee while the bee is sniffing at the pollen, also wants to be presented to its best advantage. Remember: Arranging the legs in a certain way will liven up the figure.

When spraying deep-frozen products, many fine crystals are generated on the couverture surface. Sprayed food colours stick well to this rough surface. When spraying the abdomen of the bee, you can take advantage of this fact. Cover the body with adhesive strips, spray brown food colour with the airbrush and remove adhesive strip.

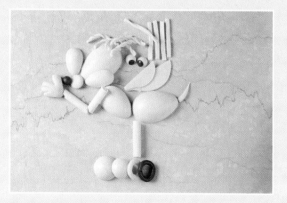

**Bee:**
Upper body and head are supported by the arm in the flower. The hair is made of twisted modelling couverture strips.

"Mmmh, the pollen smell delicious today!"

Body:        Couverture egg,
             16 x 10.4 cm / 6.29 x 4.09 in.
Head:        Couverture egg,
             14.8 x 10.3cm / 5.82 x 4.05in.
Hair:        Modelling couverture
Ears:        Couverture egg,
             4.3 x 2.6cm / 1.69 x 1.02 in.
Nose:        Couverture egg,
             6.2 x 3.8 cm / 2.44 x 1.5 in.
Eye lids:    Modelling couverture Ø = 6.5 cm / 2.55 in.
Top hat:     Couverture, moulded yoghurt glass
Hands:       Couverture egg,
             10.4 x 6.5cm / 4.09 x 2.55in.
Thumbs:      Couverture egg,
             6.2 x 3.8 cm / 2.44 x 1.5 in.
Arms:        Couverture pipes
Legs:        Couverture pipes
Feet:        Couverture egg,
             11 x 7.4 cm / 4.33x2.91 in.

The roof consists of three wooden chipboards. Break irregular pieces off a couverture plate and arrange in the form of slates.

The chimney sweep is put together on a cardboard roof of the same size. There are two reasons to favour this method: 1. When spraying the chimney sweep is given a different colour or structure. 2. The roof can still be used for another showpiece (see Santa Claus climbing into the chimney)

To produce the hair is the easiest thing imaginable. Cut a slit in three quarters of a rolled out piece of modelling couverture. These strips can either be arranged to a proper hairdo or in such a way that the hair looks completely dishevelled.

"Four-leaf clovers do not grow up here and I do not tolerate
any pigs on the roof. So you have to make do with me as good-luck charm."

# SANTA CLAUS

| | |
|---|---|
| Hands: | Couverture egg,<br>11 x 7.4cm / 4.33 x 2.91 in. |
| Thumbs: | Couverture egg,<br>6.2 x 3.8 cm / 2.44 x 1.5 in. |
| Head: | Couverture shell, Ø = 13.5 cm / 5.31 in. |
| Upper body: | Couverture egg,<br>10.5 x 16.3 cm / 4.13 x 6.41 in. |
| Ears: | Couverture half-shell Ø = 4.2 cm / 1.65 in. |
| Arms: | Couverture pipes |
| Cap: | Modelling couverture |
| Beard: | Modelling couverture |
| Moustache: | Modelling couverture |

I probably broke a taboo, when I used this carmat as a tool. But if the mat is new and if it is used for showpieces only, there is no reason not to do it.

In America, Santa Claus comes down the chimney. The work for this showpiece is minimal, if the roof is already prepared. The mighty and elegant beard and moustache cover a great part of the rest of the figure. The expression on the face, however, is characterized by this detail. To exactly achieve this effect, a stencil was made.

"These chimneys are getting narrower every year!
Next year I will either have to call the 'Weight Watchers' or eat less sweet Christmas biscuits."

Body:       Couverture, moulded piping bag holder
Head:       Couverture egg, 12 x 8 cm / 4.72 x 3.14 in.
Shoes:      Couverture shell, 10 x 6.7 cm / 3.93 x 2.36 in.
Soles:      Modelling couverture
            3 mm / 0.11 in. thick, grooved
            cut to a width of 1 cm / 0.39 in.
Jacket:     Modelling couverture, 2 mm / 0.08 in. thick
Apron:      Modelling couverture, 2 mm / 0.08 in. thick
Hat:        Modelling couverture, 3 mm / 0.11 in. thick, grooved
Arms:       Couverture pipe
Hands:      Modelling couverture
Nose:       Modelling couverture
Hair:       Modelling couverture
Mouth:      Melted out, size 22 nozzle
            oval form
Eyes:       Melted out, size 22 nozzle
            oval form
Praline
fork:       Genuine

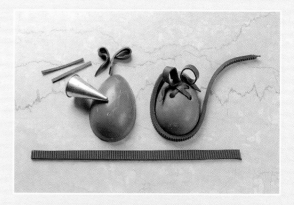

**1-hour showpiece:**
If the hollow forms are prepared, this confectioner is completed in only one hour! By slightly lifting the foot, the figure appears to be in motion.

Melt holes into the shoes using a small nozzle and pull through the shoelaces. By this or by additionally grooving the sole you will obtain even more details.

"Camera man, go on and make your picture! I'm getting cramp in my arm!"

**Rabbit:**

Body:     Couverture egg,
             16.3 x 10.5cm / 6.41 x 4.13 in.

Head:     Couverture egg, 15 x 10 cm / 5.9 x 3.93 in.

Arms:     Couverture pipes

Hands:   Couverture egg, 8.3 x 5,4 cm / 3.26 x 2.12 in.

Thumbs: Couverture egg, 6.2 x 3.8 cm / 2.44 x 1.5 in.

Cheeks: Couverture egg, 10 x 6.7 cm / 3.93 x 2.36 in.

Nose:     Couverture egg, 6.2 x 3.8 cm / 2.44 x 1.5 in.

Feet:      Couverture egg, 10 x 6.7 cm / 3.93 x 2.36 in.

Apron:    Modelling couverture

Legs:      Couverture pipes

**Bird**

Body:     Couverture egg,
             8.3 x 5.4 cm / 3.26 x 2.12 in.

Head:     Couverture shell, Ø = 6 cm / 2.36 in.

Beak:     Couverture, moulded mask

Wings:    Modelling couverture

Legs:      Couverture pipes

Eyes:      Truffle shells

Hair:      Modelling couverture,
             pressed through a
             garlic press

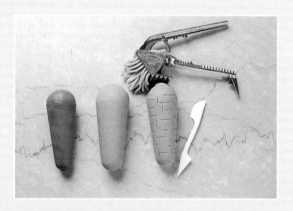

**Carrot:**

Melt a moulded champagne glass until the half-shell fits well onto it. Wrap in coloured marzipan and groove in with a modelling stick.

**Head of the Rabbit:**

Cut ears out of spread couverture and immediately lean against a chromium-steel kitchen utensil, which will result in a slight curvature of the ear.

**Bird:**

This bird is one of the author's favourite figures. The bent wings give the bird a cheeky bearing, which is even more emphasized by the big eyes.

**Straw:**

Freeze water in an aluminium sheet with borders, cover with plastic foil and pipe on the tempered couverture. Due to the temperature shock the couverture absorbs a lot of water and remains flexible for a while. Loosen couverture with a spatula and form.

"Hey, bird! Don't be offended because I do not share my snack with you!"

# RABBIT IN THE BASKET

Body:    Couverture egg,
                12 x 8 cm / 4.72 x 3.14 in.

Head:    Couverture egg,
                10 x 6.7 cm / 3.93 x 2.36 in.

Feet:    Couverture egg,
                8.3 x 5.4 cm / 3.26 x 2.12 in.

Hands:    Couverture egg, 6.2 x 3.8 cm / 2.44 x 1.5 in.

Thumbs:    Couverture egg,
                4.5 x 2.6 cm / 1.77 x 1.02 in.

Hair:    Modelling couverture

Ears:    Couverture

Cheeks:    Couverture egg, 6.2 x 3.8 cm / 2.44 x 1.5 in.,
                and couverture shell, Ø = 2.3 cm / 0.9 in.

Basket:    Couverture

Straw:    Couverture

In this case Mum's plastic table set was used. You can buy it in all department stores.

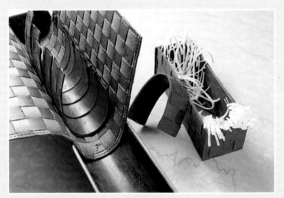

Spread couverture, cut to strips, and immediately put into a half-round baking tin that has about the same width as the basket. Make the rabbit separately and then put into the basket. Fix the handle last.

Look at the different facial expressions of the carrots.
Can this be the proof that vegetables have an inner life?

**Strawberry:** Couverture, moulded
sandbox mould
Hands: Modelling couverture
Feet: Couverture egg,
8.3 x 5.4 cm / 3.26 x 2.12 in.
Trumpet: Couverture, moulded
champagne glass

**Raspberry:** Couverture, moulded
sandbox mould
Hands: Modelling couverture
Feet: Couverture egg,
8.3 x 5.4 cm / 3.26 x 2.12 in.
and couverture shell,
Ø = 4.2 cm / 1.65 in.
Microphone: Couverture egg,
6.2 x 3.8 cm / 2.44 x 1.5 in.

**Apple:** Couverture, moulded sand-
box mould
Hands: Modelling couverture
Feet: Couverture egg,
8.3 x 5.4 cm / 3.26 x 2.12 in.
Keyboard: casted mould

**Pear:** Couverture, moulded sand-
box mould
Hands: Modelling couverture
Feet: Couverture egg,
8.3 x 5.4 cm / 3.26 x 2.12 in.
Contrabass: Modelling couverture

Forms are always deep-moulded over a coni-cal model. The model is covered with a pre-warmed plastic foil and all air bubbles are eliminated via the vacuum technique. Such deep moulds can be found in everyday life. Such moulds are cheap and ideal casting moulds for couverture.

**Sandbox moulds:**
These musicians are made of sand moulds. The base of the musicians is a deep-moulded plastic mould, which had been used to pack meat products.

Instead of spraying the fruits completely with a colour, the figure had only been shaded in a colour that indicates the type of fruit.

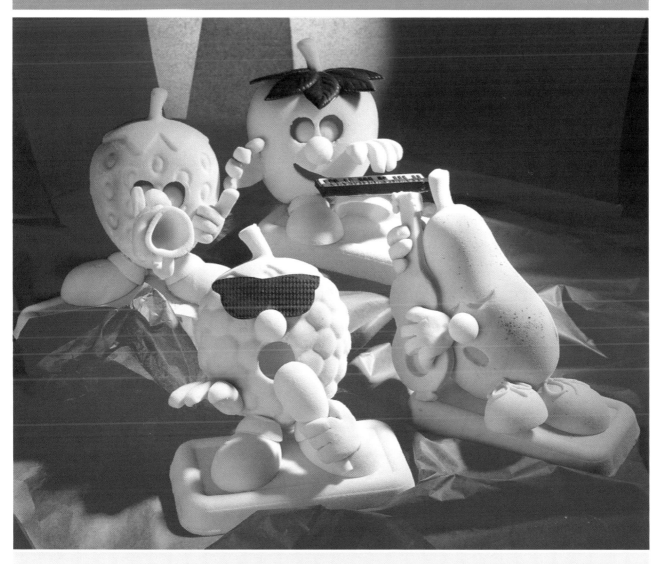

"We say hello to our German-speaking friends connected via satellite.
We are 'The Rocking Fruits' and here is a title from our
latest CD 'Picked by illegal aliens'. One, two, three, four ..."

# FISH

Fish: Couverture
Alga: Couverture strips
Bottom of Couverture spread
the sea: on a plastic sheet
Base: Hollow body of couverture
Corals: Rock sugar

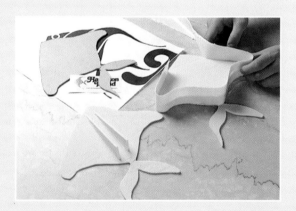

The logo used as stencil for the fish is already known through advertising.

Cut two body forms of equal size out of the couverture. Put one of these forms on the table and fix couverture strips. Put on the second fish. Spread couverture on plastic strips and wrap around the fish. Put in a cool place. Remove plastic strip and melt off protruding couverture edge. Cut out the black and white body strips and stick to the fish. Slightly spray with dark couverture.

"Bubble, bubble, bubble, bubble ...!"

# BEAR ON A HONEY-COMB

| | |
|---|---|
| Body: | Couverture egg,<br>16.3 x 10.5 cm / 6.41 x 4.13 in. |
| Head: | Couverture shell, Ø = 13.5 cm / 5.31 in. |
| Tights: | Couverture egg,<br>8.3 x 5.4 cm / 3.26 x 2.12 in. |
| Paws: | Couverture egg,<br>8.3 x 5.4 cm / 3.26 x 2.12 in. |
| Toes: | Couverture half-shells,<br>Ø = 2.3 cm / 0.9 in. |
| Muzzle: | Couverture egg,<br>8.3 x 5.4 cm / 3.26 x 2.12 in. |
| Ears: | Couverture half-shells, Ø = 5 cm / 1.97 in. |

Wrap pastry moulds in aluminium foil, cast with couverture and allow the couverture to completely crystallize. Slightly press the bottom of the aluminium upwards.

Filling the moulds with the piping bag will result in a slightly rounded paw. Pipe the heels and the toes first before you fix them.

"Caries? Who cares about caries when you face a full honey-comb!"

# GIRAFFE

| | |
|---|---|
| Legs: | Couverture, 4 moulded champagne glasses |
| Neck: | Couverture, 1 moulded champagne glass |
| Belly: | Couverture egg, 12 x 7.8 cm / 4.72 x 3.07 in. |
| Head: | Couverture egg, 10 x 6.6 cm / 3.93 x 2.59 in. |
| Muzzle: | Couverture egg, 5.4 x 8.3 cm / 2.12 x 3.26 in. |
| Ears: | Modelling couverture |
| Horns: | Modelling couverture |
| Hoof: | Half-shell, Ø = 4.2 cm / 1.65 in. |
| Mouse: | Marzipan |

The brown half-shells are used as hoofs. The moulded champagne glasses were stuck together by melting, which increases the stability. The typical spots of the giraffe had been fixed prior to spraying.

The lower egg shell of the muzzle is moved backwards by melting. This allows you to attach an exaggerated muzzle in front of it. The eye brows of modelling couverture give the eyes a more intensive expression, more profoundness and life.

"If you don't stop pulling my horns, I will throw you off and you can walk!"

# ORANGUTAN

Body:     Couverture egg, 12 x 8 cm / 4.72 x 3.14 in.
Head:     Couverture egg, 12 x 8 cm / 4.72 x 3.14 in.
Muzzle:   Couverture egg, 10 x 6.7 cm / 3.93 x 2.36 in.
Ears:     Couverture half-shell,
          Ø = 5 cm / 1.97 in.
Hands:    Modelling couverture
Feet:     Modelling couverture
Arms:     Couverture pipes
Hair:     Modelling couverture

Marzipan figures are best suited to create counterpoles: The little figures nicely accentuate the large chocolate figures. Did his grin get bigger when the camera closed in on him?

**Orangutan:**
The broad eyebrows give the eyes of the ape more profoundness. For the muzzle the two egg shells are strongly melted which results in a longer muzzle.

"I itch all over! Perhaps I should take my hairdresser's advice and try Head and Shoulders."

| | |
|---|---|
| Body: | Couverture egg, 8.3 x 5.4 cm / 3.26 x 2.12 in. |
| Head: | Couverture shell, Ø = 6 cm / 2.36 in. |
| Tights: | Modelling couverture, 12 g / 0.42 oz. |
| Feet: | Modelling couverture, 12 g / 0.42 oz. |
| Ears: | Couverture half-shell, Ø = 2.3 cm / 0.9 in. |
| Muzzle: | Couverture half-shell, Ø = 4.2 cm / 1.65 in. |
| Nose: | Modelling couverture, 2 g / 0.07 oz. |
| Tail: | Modelling couverture, 2 g / 0.07 oz. |
| Cap: | Marzipan, 15 x 6 x 6 cm / 5.90 x 2.36 x 2.36 in. |

The little Teddy bears enliven the atmosphere and gives colour to the dark showpiece with the elegant but somewhat static star. The bears are sprayed separately and then placed on the star.

Before you set about producing a showpiece, sketch your idea first. This will help you to picture the figure and to acknowledge the proportions. The time spent for drawing can thus be made up many times over, because it is much easier to work according to a model.

"Do you know why we are called Teddy bears?
The then President of the United States of America, Theodor 'Teddy' Roosevelt
refused to shoot a young bear. Since that time we are called Teddy bears."

# WORKING DRAWINGS

All but one of shown working drawings are shown in their original size. Thus no time gets lost for reducing or enlarging the working drawings.

If you want to use these stencils for your own use it is recommended to copy the following pages and to make cardboard or plastic stencils.

With these drawings and the appropriate instructions it will be a child's play for you to please your regular customers with new chocolate figures and to attract new customers.

It pays to try!

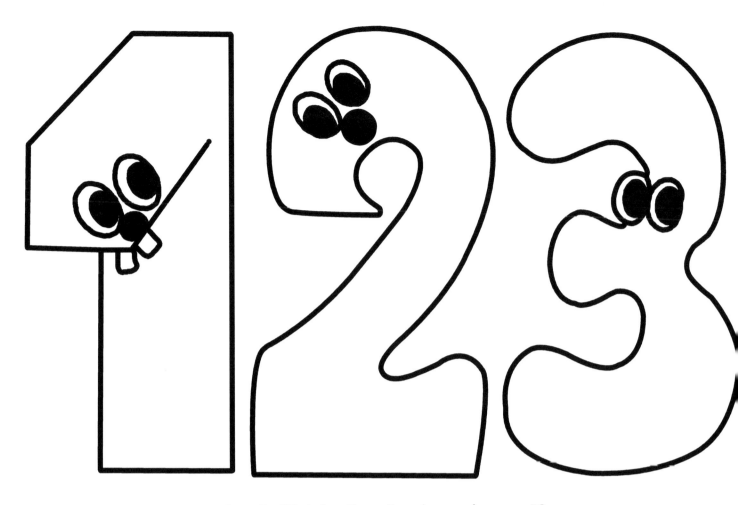

Stencils "Birthday Figure", series products, p. 52

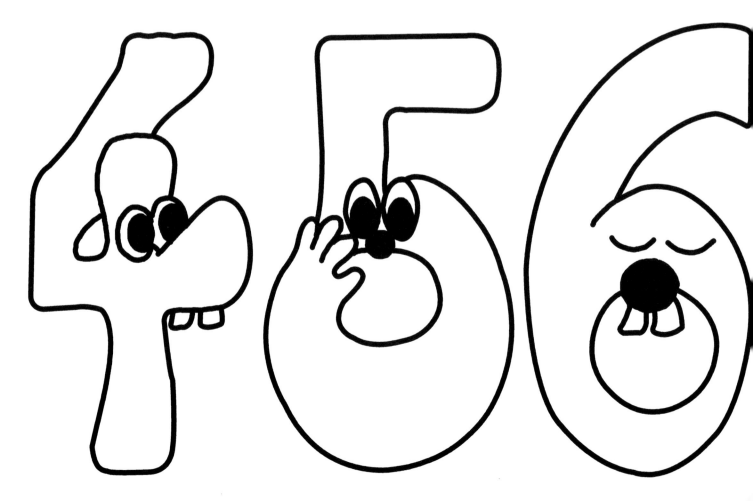

Stencils "Birthday Figure", series products, p. 52

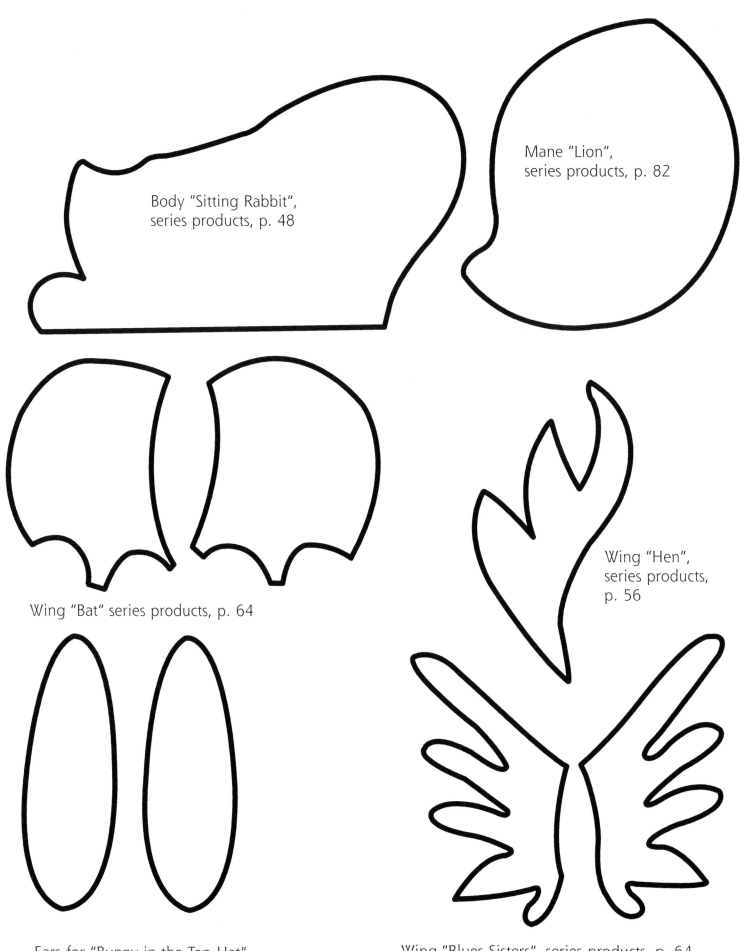

Body "Sitting Rabbit",
series products, p. 48

Mane "Lion",
series products, p. 82

Wing "Bat" series products, p. 64

Wing "Hen",
series products,
p. 56

Ears for "Bunny in the Top Hat",
series products, p. 38

Wing "Blues Sisters", series products, p. 64

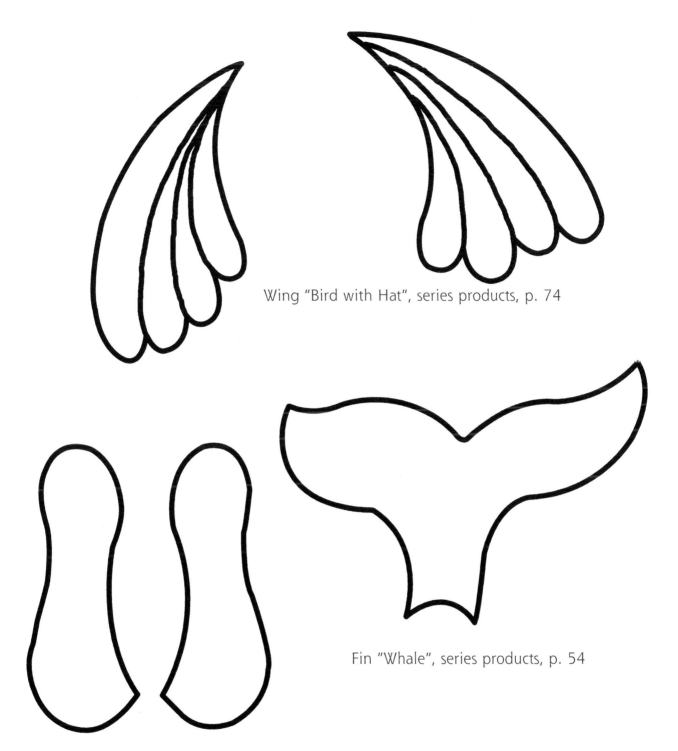

Wing "Bird with Hat", series products, p. 74

Fin "Whale", series products, p. 54

Ears "Elephant", series products, p. 66

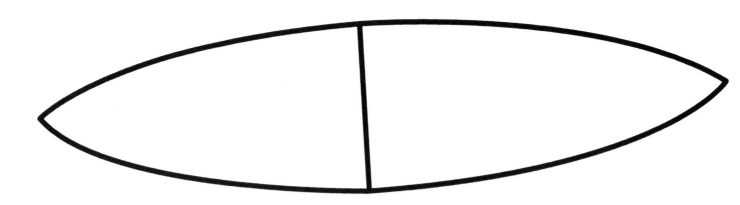

Ears for "James Bunny 007", series products, p. 40

Body "Swiss Cow", series products, p. 56

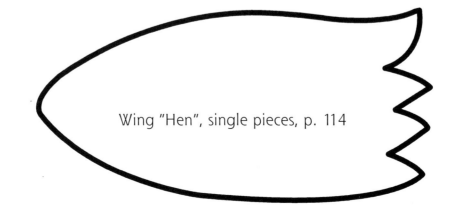

Wing "Hen", single pieces, p. 114

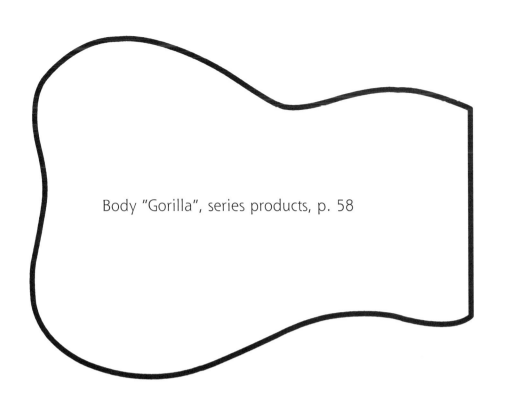

Body "Gorilla", series products, p. 58

Wing "Bee", showpiece, p. 150

Wing "Bee", showpiece, p. 150

Wing "Penguin", single pieces, p. 102

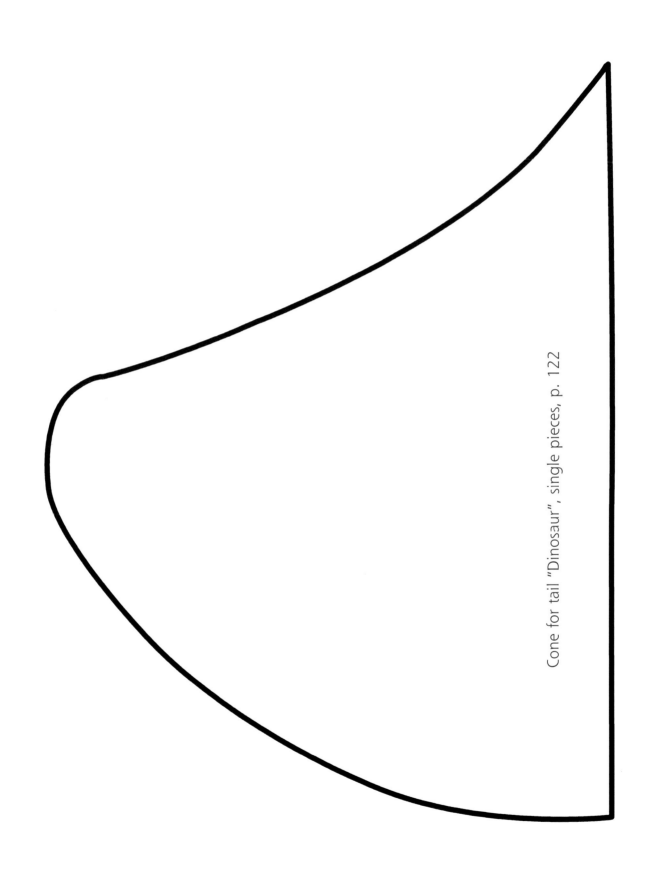

Cone for tail "Dinosaur", single pieces, p. 122

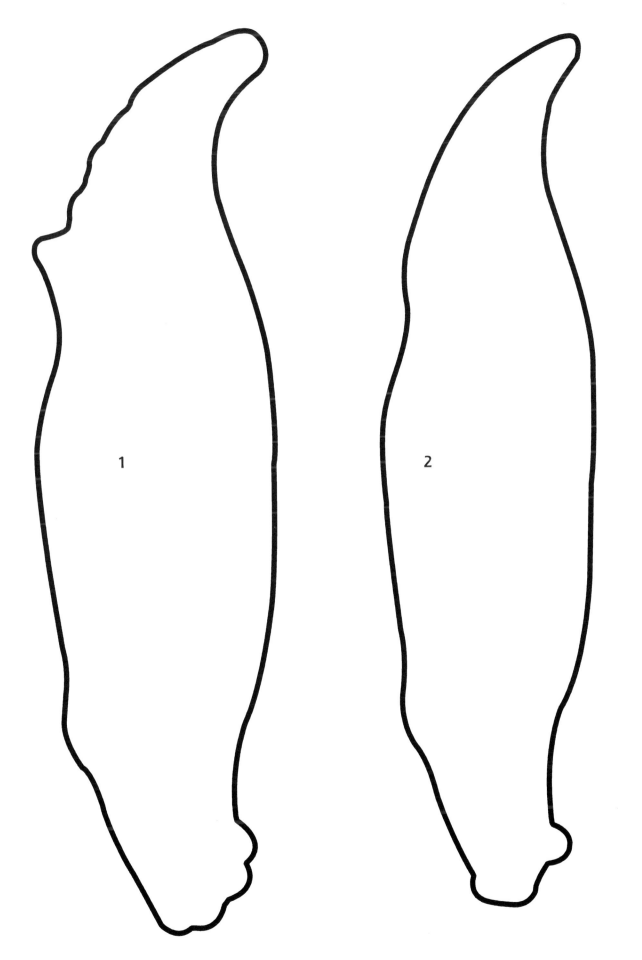

1

2

Body parts "Whales", showpieces, p. 132

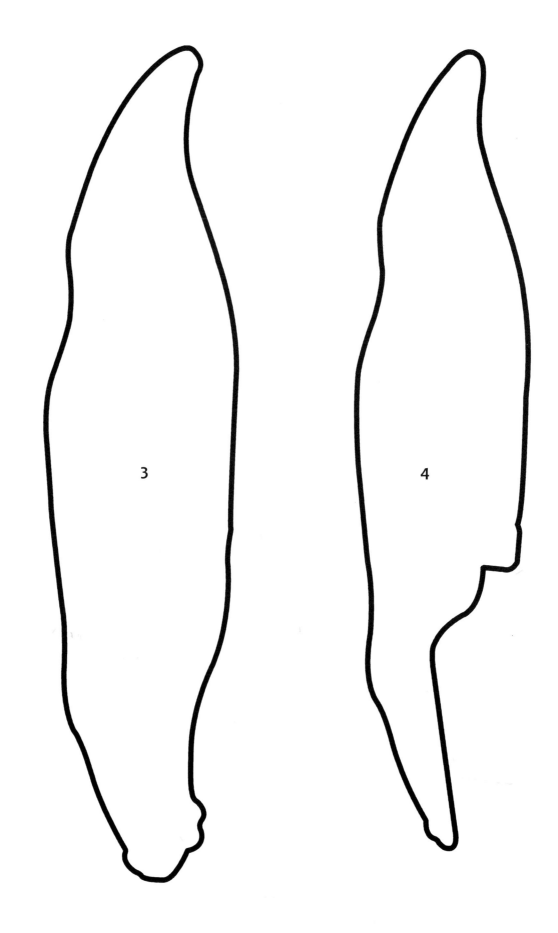

Body parts "Whales", showpieces, p. 132

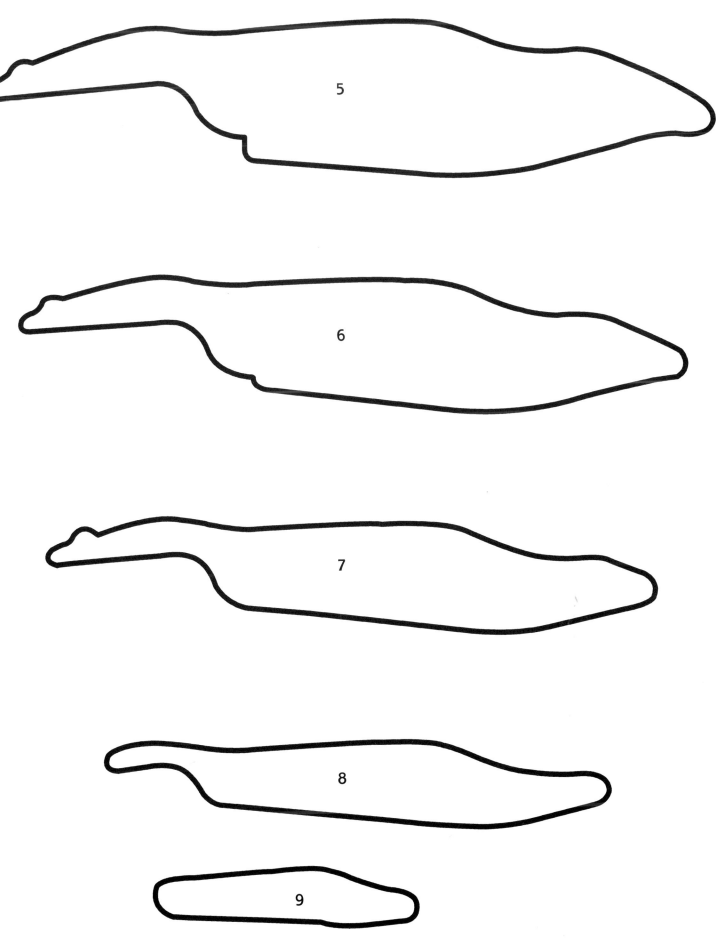

Body parts "Whales", showpieces, p. 132

Body parts "Whales", showpieces, p. 132

"Fish", showpieces, p. 164

Moustache "Santa Claus", showpieces, p. 154

Beard "Santa Claus", showpieces, p. 154

(this illustration is 90 % of the original size)

# List of suppliers

Latex, Modelling material:
Craftwork shop

Harlequin masks:
Craftwork shop

Gypsum statues:
Craftwork shop

Relief animal pictures:
Craftwork shop

Structured plexiglass:
Hardware shop

Band iron:
Hardware shop

Embossed wallpaper:
Hardware shop

Silicone rubber, RV-casting material 56:
Wacker Chemie GmbH
Hanns-Seidel-Platz 4
D-81737 München

Cold spray:
Chemist's shop

Titanium dioxide/Maser Boy (rubber for veining):
Patrick Weiss
Konditorei- und Bäckereibedarf GmbH
Tränkebachstrasse 30
CH-8712 Stäfa

Foils with different patterns:
Bombasei AG
Stationsstrasse 27
CH-8606 Nänikon

Foils with different patterns:
Chocoprint AG
Krebsgasse 26
CH-5630 Muri

Piping bag holder:
Thermo Hauser
Erwin Busch
Plastikgeräte
Postfach 49
D-73066 Uhingen

Piping bag holder:
Max Felchlin AG
Bahnhofstrasse 63
CH-6430 Schwyz

Forms for cut pralines:
Max Felchlin AG

Felchlin products are available
from the following suppliers:

**USA:**
Northwestern Region:
The Peterson Co.
1102 D.St. NE.
Auburn, WA 98002

Southwestern Region:
Swiss Chalet Fine Foods West, Inc.
8956 Sorensen Avenue
Santa Fe Springs, CA 90670-2639

Central Region:
Mid-West Imports, Ltd.
1121 South Clinton Street
Chicago, IL 60607-4416

Eastern Region:
E.A. Tosi and Sons Co., Inc.
77 Messina Drive
Braintree, MA 02184-0265

Central Southwestern Region:
Swiss Chalet Fine Foods, Inc.
7200 Wynnpark
Houston, Texas 77008-6030

Southern Region:
Swiss Chalet Fine Food, Inc.
9455 N.W. 40th Street Road
Miami, Florida 33178-2016

New York Metro Area:
Walker Foods, Inc.
66 Fadem Road
Springfield, NJ 07081

**Malaysia:**
Pastry Pro Sdn Bhd
8, Jalan 3/37A, Industrial Area
Taman Bukit Maluri
Kepong, 52100 Kuala Lumpur, Malaysia

**Australia:**
Top Shelf Food
47a Karnak Road
Ashburton, Vic. 3147
Australia

**UK:**
Döhler (UK) Ltd.
4 Vincent Avenue
Crownhill Business Centre
Milton Keynes
Bucks. MK8 0AB

**Singapore:**
Culina Pte Ltd
Alexandra Distripark Block 3
#05-30/34 Pasir Panjang Road
Singapore 0511

## Subject index

# Product index